Finding Rowland's Hut

Ann Chandler

RB
Rossendale Books

Published by Lulu Enterprises Inc.
3101 Hillsborough Street
Suite 210
Raleigh, NC 27607-5436
United States of America

Published in paperback 2015
Category: Memoirs
Copyright Ann Chandler © 2015

ISBN: 978-1-326-42063-5

All rights reserved, Copyright under Berne Copyright Convention and Pan American Convention. No part of this book may be reproduced, stored in a retrieval system, or transmitted in any form or by any means, electronic, mechanical, photocopying, recording or otherwise, without prior permission of the author. The author's moral rights have been asserted.

*In memory of Rowland who,
In flinging wide the door of his Hut,
Shared his home, his happiness, himself,
His hope in God and a desire to help his friends,
Those travelling companions of faith he met along The Way.*

This book is dedicated to my Benetton husband, whose folding and unfolding of the contents of our lives has enabled me to fiddle.

However, unlike Nero, Rome - or in this case Home, thankfully didn't burn!

Contents

Foreword 7

Introduction 9

Chapter 1: The Long and Winding Road 13

Chapter 2: Who'd Like To Be In America? 42

Chapter 3: Here Come The Girls 60

Chapter 4: Long Live Joie de Vivre 76

Chapter 5: With A Little Help From My Friend 92

Chapter 6: The Rose Of Sharon 121

Chapter 7: Who Writes The Songs? 131

Chapter 8: Carol Says 143

Chapter 9: It's A Load Of Old Conkerers! 161

Chapter 10: Tying Up The Loose Ends 173

Foreword

As you begin to turn the pages of this book, you will discover that they contain the story of my life. So far, so ordinary! However, there is an overarching, unifying theme that runs through it, namely that of "Rowland's Hut", and something that is far from ordinary. It should bring hope to the hearts of all people, resonating deeply within those who want to belong, to give and receive care, to see each other as equals, and to walk together in faith. We all need somewhere to go, people with whom we can share friendship, to be joined in a common purpose, and to be given a sense of security and significance. To be sanctified in the Christian sense means to find a place of acceptance and rest, to be touched by God, and protected by Him. My definition of Rowland's Hut would be to describe it as a place of sanctuary, either physical or spiritual, where those who feel in danger, or who feel lost, or lonely, can find protection, shelter, and acceptance. We can all think of times when we needed either physical provision, or spiritual support, or both!

I once experienced homelessness - briefly, fleetingly, temporarily. As a young girl in a foreign, but highly civilised land, I, along with my mother and brother, suffered the trauma of being expelled from the home of relatives we'd been visiting. Left with facing the fear, and the emotional stress of displacement and dispossession, it's something you would never want anyone to go through, but regrettably it happens - every day, in every way, in every town, village, and country, and to every type of person. The gulf between homelessness and owning a home seems to be widening amongst the displaced of the world. In my case, we were immediately rescued by the kindness of strangers, who took us into their homes, and made sure we were looked after, until the date of our departure. With hindsight, the provision of that particular "Rowland's Hut", at a time of shock and disbelief that this had happened to me, was the most important of my life. I now need to let this impact my attitude towards the dispossessed and the disenfranchised, the refugee, and the political prisoner. Perhaps the most obvious are the homeless on our streets, who are right under our own noses. I want to learn not to "pass by" and to be unafraid to buy that hot drink, that sandwich, that carton of soup, to give that coin, or to engage with them in their struggles. In the blink of an eye, it could so easily be me again, but with far more reaching effects than my previous experience, having to learn not to judge, or jump to wrong conclusions. After all, wasn't it Jesus who said that to do something small for the least is to do it for Him?

In seeking to locate those times in my own life when I'd received provision, I've recalled much physical, emotional, and spiritual help, freely given in times of personal crisis. I owe much to many, and hope that I, in turn, can offer the support and shelter of a Rowland's Hut, in which others can sit, hide, recover, and become strong again to face life's battles.

Introduction

Home Is Where The Heart Lies.

"Though he with giants fight, he will make good his right to be a pilgrim."
- John Bunyan

Once upon a time, there was a giant called Rowland. He wanted to live in a mysterious Hut he'd discovered deep in the forest, and which was very near to The Big House. Some Fearsome, Feathered Creatures had seized the Hut for themselves, and if anyone tried to take it over, the creatures would fly at them, pecking their eyes out with their huge beaks. However, Rowland was a fearless and determined giant, and decided he wanted the Hut for himself, so in threatening to ring the necks of the Fearsome Feathered Creatures and put them in boiling water, they all ran away, squawking and shaking their feathers. Rowland became the King of the Hut, holding court on his throne. Being a gentle giant, he soon made friends with The Little People, and started to invite them into his Hut. Rowland had lots of treasures around him, but he never had to worry that the Little People would ever take anything away, because he trusted them. He made them feel warm and welcome, and they loved being his friend. Rowland and The Little People had a Big Friend who could see them, but they couldn't see him - at least, not with their eyes. The Big Friend had hidden himself, but it wasn't going to be forever. They all sang and laughed and talked to each other, as well as to their invisible Big Friend. They loved each other and would do anything for each other. They all lived happily ever after.

When you finish a fairy story, you close the book, kiss your little one "Goodnight" and tiptoe down the stairs. However, this is no fairy story, but a real life story! It's about a real Rowland, a real Hut, and a real group of people (though not all of them little!). Rowland was a young man who, for reasons best known to himself, had moved out of the family house, (The Big House). He had taken up residence in the garden, living happily in a large Hut that had once been a chicken shed (the home of the Fearsome, Feathered creatures). Rowland helped lead a Christian gathering of young, and not so young, folk (the Little People), who belonged to a group called The Squash - that really was its name, honest! On Sunday evenings, he opened the Hut to his friends so that they could be together to worship God (the Big Friend). The throne was Rowland's bed, which doubled as a sofa on which numerous others would sit, owing to a shortage of chairs! The treasures were his collection of antiques and Other Objects (!), arranged with, let's say, carefree abandon around the Hut! The warmth was partly due to the old stove they sat round, but mainly because of his warm welcome and the opportunity he afforded others to meet with God. A devotee of those Hut days recalled this nutshell impression: It was "full of bric-a-brac and several threadbare carpets. Also, a rather comfy single bed. Seem to remember dozing off on it!". A happy bunny, then!

As we travel on our life journey, there are times when we feel like the giant - fearless, determined, invincible, able to cope well, our lives ascending like an escalator. We can be so self contained that we don't need to relate or to rely on others. However, when someone presses the stop button on the escalator, we come to a juddering halt. We become like the Little People - not those of the fairy story, with their trust and happiness, but "little" in the sense of our shrinking emotional and spiritual stature. What do we do, where can we turn to, who can we turn to? We can turn to God, finding He's been there all the time, waiting to help us find those who will accept us and love us.

I was in a well known clothes store recently, and in trying to find a quiet spot where I could wait for my husband, who was in the changing rooms, I found myself standing in a stairwell, just off the beaten track of frantic shoppers. Attached to the wall was a button, encased in a glass cover, with an accompanying picture of a wheelchair and a message reading "refuge point" placed above both. I immediately thought of Rowland's Hut, and how it had been a point of refuge for those disabled in spirit, anyone needing help, and for anyone who just wanted to belong in an atmosphere of love and acceptance - in other words, everyone! As Sting (one of my music and word-smith heroes!) says in his song, "With one roof above our heads, a warm house to return to". Who, in a relational sense, wouldn't want that?

It just goes to show that good things don't just have to happen in fairy stories! I hope you'll be inspired and encouraged to seek out places and people in your life where you can be accepted for just being yourself. We all need to feel affirmation from others - to help us believe we're an "okay" person, with value and a place in this sometimes (often!) lonely world, and going a long way in helping us to trust that God thinks we're "okay". As a matter of fact, He thinks we're more than "okay" - He thinks each one of us is special, precious, unique! We need to remember that, although we know we "know only in part" at the moment, ONE DAY, "WE SHALL KNOW, EVEN AS WE ARE KNOWN"!

It really doesn't matter how you choose to read the following contents. Like the name that runs through the middle of a stick of seaside rock, and wherever you happen to "bite", you'll come across Rowland, and his Hut! I hope you'll feel encouraged to find your own Rowland's Hut in such a fragile world.

Chapter 1: The Long and Winding Road

"Don't leave me standing here, lead me to your door."
- Paul McCartney

As a little girl, it soon became clear that my modus operandi (the posh way of saying how I went about things) was to think and act in black and white, very straight lines. Organisation was an automatic and easy process for me. In fact, my junior school headmistress, who, incidentally had also taught my father, described me as being able to organise her! There was no room for mental cul de sacs and the way was always forward, but that didn't mean I wasn't lateral in my thinking. When travelling home from Scotland with a group of friends, a delay in our journey meant we were going to be quite late in our arrival. Who was the one who hit on the idea of phoning our home railway station to ask for a message to be put out for our parents? However, I didn't linger in mental highways and byways but moved on, much like a conveyor belt. If I'd allowed some detours to feature in my thinking, I would have had somewhere to go - a bolt hole, a pink and fluffy "girl" place, a Rowland's Hut in which to hide from those icy fingers of fear that used to grip my heart on Sunday evenings. The root of this anxiety was primary school arithmetic, this nursery slope being replaced at a later date by the Mount Everest of senior school mathematics! Sunday nights would be spent in a state of rigid fear, reducing my mathematical performance to a place not only "a little lower than the angels" but in the underworld of shame and humiliation. I didn't do myself any favours with my no-

nonsense, sergeant major approach, not at that stage, anyway. It was, however, eminently successful in teaching, that lion taming career of all careers. This is when I came into my own - and possibly everyone else's! Here was my stage! This is where my captive audience WOULD play its part in my play, WOULD listen to my stage directions in standing up, sitting down, folding its collective arms and laying down its arms of disobedience. They WOULD become my model army....

Life, that existential state, was to teach me that there were bends in the straight lines and curves in the paths, despite my best efforts to keep them ironed out. I was to discover that roads were to prove long and winding. Now, where have I heard that before? I had never had a problem with God, at least, not in believing He was there. No, the problems I had were to do with a conscience that wouldn't lie down and go to sleep, doing the things I shouldn't have done, and not doing the things I should have done. The giant I wrestled with was over not wanting to go to Africa as a missionary! Our friend, on the other hand, would still jump at the chance to go, wanting to drive and deliver a tractor to some deserving community. It's a truly noble aim, but I do hope he realises there's the small matter of crossing some ocean. Perhaps he thinks that, like the Children of Israel, the sea will part and onward he'll trundle! Anyway, I constantly pleaded with God not to send me there, or possibly not anywhere. I seem to have got away with it so far, remaining parochial but hopefully not small minded. Oh yes - there was just one more thing. I used to wish that God would find another method of recording my attendance at Sunday School, other than the register. There was the bright idea of each child having to take it in turns to fill it in. I'm drawing a veil over an activity I would now regard as technology, therefore needing a flag with a skull and crossbones flying above it. I've filed it away under the categories marked Embarrassing, Miserable and Failure. It has to be admitted that later, as a teacher, my registers were not exactly pristine!

In talking about Sunday School and straight lines, strong memories have been evoked of what I shall sub-title my "Blancmange and Bluebells" days. Despite that very threatening prospect of having to fill in the register, (a bit like swimming in shark infested seas!), I still relied on my weekly attendance as being the plumb line to my existence, a straight connection to my centre of gravity. However, in all the years of my earnest and shiny faced attendance, I never once qualified for a book prize at the annual Anniversary presentation, an act that seemed inexplicably cruel then and even now. It was all judged on a "points make prizes" basis, awarded for the qualifying number of attendances, which I always failed to attain, and for which no allowances were made for "circumstances beyond our control", a phrase that used to be announced by the BBC when the screen went haywire. Well, my "screen" did exactly the same, when, at the drop of a hat, I'd have to miss Sunday School in order to perform that Sunday afternoon ritual, the family country car ride, designed especially with my Grandma in mind. No one realised the huge cul de sac it made in my straight line living, or perhaps even considered that it mattered to me, being of the "seen and not heard", "cleanliness is next to Godliness", "keep off the grass" generation! I certainly felt that, as a member of Sunday School, I was The Spiritual Black Sheep, regarded as always straying beyond the fence and bunking off to paddle in a stream (if sheep do such things), whilst The Virtuous strode across the platform, clutching their book prizes in triumph. There goes another life lesson - right person, wrong time, wrong place, Game, Set and Match!

After overcoming the feeling that the wheels were taking me away from my chosen destination, I resigned myself to being wedged like an unwilling book end, in the back of the "state of the art" Morris minor car, its leather seats cold and stiff. We passed by the burgeoning car factories, those post war city glittering prizes (not fair, even they had some - prizes, that is!), leaving behind the familiarity of the buildings, in order to seek out a rural idyll. If only I'd realised at the time that God was indeed as much with me in the green and pleasant countryside as He would have been in Sunday School. On winding through country lanes that whispered a promise in my ear, it was delivered on arrival at some leafy glade, copse or suitable field. The little wooden chairs (and if I'm being totally honest, the rather dubious toilet of Sunday School) were forgotten as we decanted the contents of the boot onto the now familiar picnic rug.

My excitement began to rise when I glimpsed the assorted picnic bags, knowing that my Grandma, who ran a little grocery shop with my Grandad, (who never seemed to figure in my Sunday afternoon memories - probably minding the shop), would have provided food of the proverbial finest fare. For me, the highlight was the blancmange, a pink and slightly wobbly creation in its mould, accompanied by tinned - yes, delicious, but tinned, raspberries! If not theologically Heaven, it certainly was the equivalent of its famous Manna! With the future picnic reassuringly secured in my mind, it was time to hunt the seasonal floral treasures, the most iconic being those of my "Blancmange and Bluebells" opening phrase. Coming across a densely carpeted area of bluebells was a magical, heart stopping moment, the bell shaped flowers holding an almost fairy-like fascination for me, and always linked to Sunday outings with Grandma. Later, full of blancmange and raspberries, I would be allowed to pick some of the choice flowers, roll them gently in newspaper, and transport them home, to adorn some window sill for a day or two before they drooped.

My day had been turned on its axis, having become a lusciously pink and ravishingly blue rainbow of compensation. It typified what I now see as God's reward, His Rowland's Hut for the rude interruption to my social and spiritual routine. Who needed a book, anyway? Being retrospective has helped me realise that "redeeming the time the locusts had eaten" had actually taken place, removing the no-mark of my Sunday School shame and my seeming irrelevance to that happy band of childhood pilgrims. What of my replacement prizes? They were as long lasting and life affirming as sitting on a little wooden seat, in a little wooden church hall, waiting for Mr. Bailey and Mr. Wyman, the superintendents, to notice little eager me sitting in front of them, year in and year out. Although my heart belonged to Sunday School and everyone there, I'm not sure if it, and they, belonged to me. More to the point, their arbitrary rules didn't make me feel included in the Rowland's Hut they were supposed to be providing. Despite that disappointment, I hold onto those years with gratefulness, knowing they were God's purposes for me. I shall always be grateful to my friend's mum, who had persuaded my mum - that word of mouth thing, to let me go to Sunday School with her daughter. It was my introduction to the God who has always had me in His sight, and who made a pathway for me, mainly straight, sometimes curved, but always firm, rather like the long road between home and Sunday School, and trying to please those people at either end!

I continued travelling along my straight and certain route until I experienced a revelation, the one that stopped me in my tracks, causing me to do a U-turn. It was of such magnitude that it sent the needle on my inner compass spinning round, not knowing where to come to rest. It was a Eureka moment, the pieces of the family jigsaw suddenly falling into place. It appeared that I was a descendant of a Jewish White Russian family. This particular cat was out of the bag in which it had remained hidden, family members frantically trying to push it back in, but it was too late - I'd seen it! The momentous news resonated deep within me and started to make sense of random events that had been lodged in my memory. So, some of the blood coursing through my veins was my direct line to Abraham, The Father of All Nations.

My back catalogue of thoughts began to rearrange and update themselves, and as a result, I became much more informed by the genealogical turn of events. A clue as to my Grandpa's background was his unusual vocabulary, perceived as entirely normal and having been absorbed into the family's everyday life. I now know that, along with everyone else, I had imbibed Yiddish (some, at any rate) - the form of German spoken by the Ashkenazim Jews of Eastern Europe. This was the language of my Great Grandparents, who'd come to England from Belarus in the mid nineteenth century. I'm not sure whether they would have approved of the more dubious version my Grandpa had adopted, many words and expressions needing the censure's blue pencil through them! At one point, I wouldn't necessarily have been able to tell whether he was speaking English, Yiddish or rubbish, such were his skills as a raconteur and his ability to mesmerise! Maybe that's why the stage and performance element of teaching appealed to me. I began to see my Grandpa's friends and acquaintances in a new light, colourful Jewish characters, governed by inherent characteristics of their Eastern European Jewish roots, perceptibly different but hard to articulate. On a personal level, I realised why Jewish music resonated so deeply within me, so much so that I used it as the subject of my special study at college.

Armed with this new information about my background, I had the pleasure of meeting Nick Howard, an itinerant evangelical Christian. He's the son of politician Michael Howard, a practising Jew, with a Romanian Jewish father and a Jewish mother. In talking to Nick, I discovered to my surprise that even with my diluted blood, I could become a citizen of Israel - should I want to! Now, I happen to know several "wannabe Jews" who would jump at the chance. Those of a romantic nature try to re-invent themselves into Jewishness by a form of spiritual osmosis. They specialise in changing their names into those Hebrew sounding ones that truly Jewish people have spent their lives disguising! I'm left wondering if it's some mental fast track to holiness. However, there's nothing romantic about the fear and indignity suffered by countless thousands down the years. Jewishness is not a theme park, where those with a passing fancy can play.

As for me, I had inherited a portion of the real deal, a valid blood bond bequeathed by my maternal family line. The Jack was out of The Box! A mystery had been solved that I didn't even know I was looking for, concerning people I didn't even know had existed. My great grandparents, along with thousands of others were desperately determined to escape their deprivation and threat of death under nineteenth century Tsarist persecution. They were herded onto ships (someone supposedly having guaranteed their passage), and hoping that they were being transported to the new Promised Land of their dreams. In the case of my great grandparents and many others, they were short changed, the currency not being the dollars and dimes of

America but the pounds and pence of Britain. Their unceremonious disembarkation would have been in Hull, with their final destination being Leeds. Not exactly scattered with the stardust of the States, it nevertheless offered them the safety and stability a million miles away from the danger, if not the annihilation that has historically been the lot of The Chosen Race.

My mother had not been brought up to fully understand or to embrace either the implications of her mixed background - Jewish father, Gentile mother or indeed her relations themselves. Nevertheless she had stored up her memories and impressions and has passed on her bird's eye view, her descriptions having acted like a powerful magnet on my senses and imagination. Her tales of her grandmother, a tiny, wrinkled foreign lady cooking fish on an open fire and of smart men in dark overcoats and homburg hats knocking at the door of the off-the-street dwelling painted an intriguing picture. I wasn't privileged to know my great grandmother, but I did know her son, my grandfather, an exotic, quixotic character. It didn't take much encouragement for him to turn into a dazzling peacock, a raconteur, a Jewish song-and-dance boy as were so many of his background. He was like Joseph's Coat, having many facets to his being, and adopting a variety of names to suit the occasion, whether war or peace, Sunday or Friday, friend or foe! Name change, of course was a basic and very biblical principal. He certainly had a hatful of them. He also had an acerbic wit and a typically characteristic dry humour mixed with truth. As my beloved Grandpa used to say "they promised us the earth - they gave us Fuller's earth!" Well, "they" did, didn't "they"? I've absorbed other pearls of Yiddish wisdom, (this having been his mother tongue), highly entertaining, mostly dubious and certainly unmentionable here.

However, this kind of expression was inherited from a people who had to have sheer grit and foresight just to survive. Transported not to the Land of the Free and Home of the Brave that was America (every Jewish wish), but to Britain, they indeed were the brave ones!

My Great Grandparents, Abraham and Annie, (names probably Anglicised) were two young things who had been stripped of their status, trade and familiarity of home. The climate for Jews was extremely dangerous in Russia in the eighteen hundreds, so they were prepared to be herded like cattle onto ships bound for wherever, but preferably America, with no spoken English, a name change and a culture shock awaiting them. They came, they saw and they tried to conquer and my heart and admiration goes out to them. I never knew them, but then again, I feel I do. I know them through their offspring, through the family oral legacy, from the epitaphs on their gravestones, and for just having existed. Until recent times, Jewish gravestones contained the names of the fathers, but this practice is now disappearing. What is truly amazing in the case of my great-grandfather is that his gravestone also bears the names of my great, great and great, great, great grandfathers! How wondrous is that? I've managed to find their resting places where they lie amongst the Chosen People of East European Jewry. The Hebrew burial places appear to all the world like an unending flock of migrating birds, which is exactly what they were, their flight to freedom actually having been by boat, the circumstances being less than adequate for human dignity. There's the great and the small, the good, the bad and the very possibly ugly, the first Jewish lawyer of Leeds lying next to a butcher from Belarus. My Great Grandfather shares his Big Sleep alongside a relation of the actress and film star, Gwyneth Paltrow. She and her family managed to achieve the goal of getting to America, the hope shared by east European Jews and half of the underdeveloped world alike. She may have been fulfilling a subconscious promise made on behalf of those whose hearts had desired to get there, but hadn't been able to. In reality, one of her parents married an American so she was actually born there, her successful career as an actress, probably a by-product of her life as an American. To know and be known has always been a prime need of humans, whatever the background and origin. It has come to mind that one of my great grandparents' daughters emigrated from England to America and subsequently had a daughter of her own. She must have been a dark haired "looker", becoming a beauty queen in one of the ubiquitous competitions beloved by that great melting pot of a continent. Those "Jews Of The Boat", whose remains are lying in the ground in British and other burial places, all foreign when compared to their original homeland, are in a category all of their own. They take your breath, and any shoddy sense of superiority, completely away. These Children of Abraham were, and still are, estranged from their homeland but more poignantly, from Israel, the land of their intention, the land God had promised would be theirs through the obedience of their Patriarch. Once again, it had been necessary for a group of dispossessed Jews to journey across a desert, a slightly more civilised desert than the one of the Forty Year traipse, but a land that was alien nevertheless. I do hope they found the comfort of a Rowland's Hut amongst the challenge of strangeness.

A "who dunnit" story usually makes you wait until the end before all the threads are drawn together and the mystery solved. I'm choosing to buck the trend by showing my hand near the beginning! It's a sort of "leitmotif" of the literary kind, the recurring idea of Rowland's Hut that runs through this book.

The following is one of those "stranger than fiction" moments. A broadcast of "Who Do You Think You Are?", a programme that traces the ancestries of chosen celebrities, featured the Jewish family of the actress, Zoe Wanamaker. Having closely followed those appearing in the series whose roots were Russian Jewish (usually one in every series), my mother and I felt that this was the closest reflection to our own background that had been shown to date. Zoe Wanamaker discovered that her great grandparents were from Nikolyev, a little town in the Ukraine, which she visited. She experienced a sense of identity and wonder, emotions felt by those who find what they have been searching for. The programme went on to feature the typical housing that Jews in nineteenth century Russia would have lived in. On seeing the houses, Zoe exclaimed "CHICKEN SHEDS! They lived in chicken sheds!" It was heart-stopping. There, right in front of my eyes were little hut houses, similar in nature to the one Rowland had lived in! The uncanny similarity was not only significant, but prophetic. A friend described it as Serendipity, a happy accident, but it seemed to be more like a finger pointing the way. The physical image of the limited space seemed to illustrate the close knit, closely woven family life that characterized the Jewish people and which, together with their faith, helped them in their determination to survive in the face of persecution. It certainly qualifies them to be members of the type of Hut I initially described, the one desired by God for us to inhabit, in a world so often devoid of a "soft centre".

This could so easily have been the subject of a work of fiction with its unusual subject matter, but it was, as they say, stranger than fiction. To the sceptics, it would seem like a matter of coincidence - a case of the mind seizing upon material to make some nebulous, fanciful idea credible. Well, maybe so, but I doubt that even a sceptic could ignore the timing of this unlikely scenario with its unusual means of housing and thematic idea that had been crystallising in my mind. To have presented itself at the beginning of the process of writing of this book was quite a shock, a pivotal, authenticating moment, and a huge boost to continue. If you go back and check out the definition of Rowland's Hut (incidentally not mine) at the beginning of my book, you may be as surprised as I am by the incredible "life mirroring art" and "life mirroring life" factors! There, in front of my eyes was the reinforcement of my idea, the physical embodiment representing a spiritual state I had previously encountered and wanted to locate in myself and others. I leave this auspicious happening with a healthy dose of respect, wondering if genetics do rule after all? I felt I had been provided with a "nudge" to progress down the "Long and Winding Road" of discovery, much like the subject of Paul McCartney's plaintive and iconic song, whose subject was hoping to be led to the door of his or her desire. Wasn't that what I was hoping for as well?

I do hope that frying their fish on their Yorkshire fires and lighting their Shabbat candles at sunset on Fridays brought the displaced Jewish people a sense of security, continuity, and a sense of place. I hope that memories of those left behind were not so painful that it stopped their sense of moving forward. We will never know how they squared that particular circle. Many came as family groups, others not so fortunate. From my mother's recollection of her visits to her, it appeared that my great grandmother couldn't speak much, if any English, and certainly never learned to write any, signing all documents with an X. I know this to be true from the birth and death certificates I have managed to obtain. I don't know how much or how little she lived life outside her four walls, but she would have been a plucky lady to have negotiated her life without the usual intelligible props of her own country. I hope that she amounted to more than X marking the spot! I hope that God in His graciousness allowed her the presence of the Cloud and the Fiery Pillar to guide her on her life journey. As for the hope of Heaven, that's up to God, His Light and His mercy. With my great grandparents' hearts most probably broken by each of their numerous offspring doing what was known as "marrying out", (marriage to a non-Jewish partner), and considered the gravest offence, they had tried (and felt, perhaps, that they had failed) to keep this tenet of their ancient faith. As mill girls claimed their sons and America their daughters, all hopes of matches made either in Heaven or through the community maker of such matches faded, like the "Sunrise, Sunset" song in "Fiddler On The Roof".

Some strategic searching enabled me to locate the graves of both great grandparents and a great aunt who, having been brought up mainly by her great grandparents, died from a heart condition when she was nineteen. My mother, her sister, also had the same condition many years later, but was able to benefit from the development of corrective heart surgery that had become widely available. The words on my Great Grandfather's gravestone tell the names of his father, Yitchok and his grandfather, Chaim. They also indicate just how much those who loved him and worshipped with him, missed him. They tell of his proud connection with two synagogues, The Court Hope Of Israel and The Pride of Israel. Even then, that particular group of the Diaspora were watching, hoping, waiting… how could they believe so implicitly in the Mogen David while still rejecting the Son Of David? For me, it will remain a sadness and a puzzle as to their blindness, except to say that any religious system will try to keep its members confined within its creedal walls. It isn't as if Jesus wouldn't have wept over all the persecution, expulsions, exterminations and degradation that have always been the lot of those with the label "Jew". He must have thought that what comes around, goes around. In the case of my family, Tsar Nicholas had become King Herod, Pontius Pilate and assorted subversives all rolled into one. He wanted to continue the line of predators whose inhumane, racist acts of cruelty stalked to kill The Chosen, yet fallen Race. So that's the story of my bloodline inheritance and my compulsion to wander and to wonder. This pattern of wandering, looking for, searching and wondering has permeated my being, and is always prevalent at the critical junctions of my life.

From an early age, I would lean over the garden gate and accost any passing stranger with my "Hello man" greeting, not an activity to be recommended today, life obviously seeming less threatening in the nineteen forties! My need to connect with "out there" was evident from the beginning. Later on, when I had progressed beyond the confines of the gate, my wanderings were given full reign. I explored my neighbourhood with its alleyways, often in trepidation of meeting dogs (always my enemy) but undeterred in my quest for "je ne sais quoi" or in today's parlance, I dunno! Having become an avid reader, my wandering extended to the library, where an armful of books and an apple in my pocket would send me home in a state of ecstasy and with a new and exciting purpose. The need to wander would be temporarily abated as I entered into a new and totally absorbing world. However, the wanderlust soon returned, this time to the magnetic pull of the city, that new and shiny creation of post-war Britain, rising like the Phoenix out of the ashes. Perhaps the most important part of my search was the visiting of places of worship. There was Anglican with candles, Catholic with statues and even more candles, Methodist with no candles, Baptist with sloping floors, wooden pews and definitely no candles, Congregational with no sloping floors, still no candles and nothing else visually to commend it!

On the other hand, Jewish synagogues had an almost exotic appeal, the metropolitan ones being particularly opulent, the resplendent chandeliers adorning these buildings being a source of amazement to me. Growing up in a spiritual environment that owed its ambience to Calvin, finding such decorations in any House of God seemed wildly out of place. They did, however, more than make up for the absence of candles, causing me to examine the kind of God who went in for this level of grandeur. I wasn't complaining, only marvelling that I had made this discovery and that not only were they permitted but were "de rigour". They had certainly never been the order of my day, worship-wise or any-wise! On a recent programme featuring a nineteenth century synagogue in Russia, I was intrigued to see that it also had a huge ring of lights suspended from the ceiling, not exactly a chandelier as we know them, but a passable imitation and obviously a design feature that has continued in the trappings of Jewish worship life. With hindsight, my quest was now clearer than at the time of my fairly unformed and sketchily informed juvenile mind, that of trying to answer the unanswerable. It manifested itself in my searching to see if God were waiting for me in any or all of these buildings. I suppose I was hoping that it would be like the pantomime, where the audience would shout "He's behind you!" Since those earnest days of my youth (and not so youth) I came to realise that He is not only "in there" but "out there", in front, behind and everywhere we go. In fact, we think we can evade and avoid Him, but He never lets us go, even when we want Him to. God is respectful, never forcing Himself upon us, preferring to make us aware of the choice we have in acknowledging Him. We have to look beyond the candles, the statues, the chandeliers (where some like to swing!) or even the plainness, to find Him.

Having thought long and hard about this wander/wonder element to my character, I've decided that it may have come with the genetic territory. Maybe this has been transmitted through a chromosome, not scientifically detectable but present nevertheless, propelling my ancestors on escape routes down through time to destinations sympathetic enough to accept them. Perhaps this is why I can gather things together quickly, form plans at the drop of the proverbial hat, and respond to a change of direction at the speed of light! This drives other people crazy but stimulates me to rise to the challenge, and very rarely do I have to look back or worry as to whether I've locked the door or turned off the appliance, thoughts that possibly haunt others all day. However, in my case, it doesn't seem to have included a desire to go to far flung places for any length of time.

The awareness of my background has been largely retrospective, there being only one incident in my childhood that stood out, and threw me into confusion, Whilst on holiday and wandering round the empty sun washed streets of the pretty seaside town, the early morning was working its usual magic on me. However, a woman who happened to be staying at the same hotel soon broke the spell. This complete stranger accosted me with what seemed to be the strangest request, asking me to verify that I was indeed Jewish. I had no idea what she was talking about, and because I was on my own, felt very strange and very disturbed at the suggestion. I will leave you to speculate the reasons behind this encounter. True to form, my mother fudged the whole thing and the uncomfortable incident faded. However, we know that nothing actually disappears from our recording system, at least in a healthy brain. That particular memory was vivid and piercing, making me feel like I had been stripped naked in public, an exposure with no explanation. Was the woman exercising her powers of detection to attempt a brotherhood/sisterhood tribal connection? Less positively, was she trying to communicate a kind of superiority or worse still, her dislike of my apparently Jewish presence? At eleven years old, even Miss-Know-It-All didn't actually know it all and knew nothing of racial distrust. After all, wasn't it me who demanded conversation and sociability from all and sundry over the garden gate of my infancy? I was no discriminator - I just wanted to talk!

As an adult, I now realise that the extended family refused to acknowledge the whole topic of its background, having experienced quite a degree of what should be termed persecution. Neighbourhood accusations such as "dirty gypsies" were made, scarring all concerned and causing my grandfather to retaliate, understandably so. One such occasion saw him taking off his belt, threatening to use it on the accuser, and ending up in a fight, costing both families their rented homes. This scenario has a familiar ring to it, there certainly being no room at the inn! It was at this point that my grandmother made the decision that she would, in future, own her own home. Even though these incidents were indelible in her memory, the deepest aspects of the cause were not really perceived by my mother and her siblings. The whole thing was driven underground and replaced with a layer of "respectability" which, of course produced denial. Now, this is totally understandable when survival is paramount, and when racial hatred is always being in your face. Regrettably, it doesn't cater for the richness of character that can be gained from another ethnic background or, perhaps, traits and characteristics which otherwise could not be explained. It can produce a kind of "Hitler from within" effect, diluting, if not expunging, a whole bloodline. I suppose the feeling of shame thrust upon them all was too high a price to pay, taking into account their mother was a Gentile and indeed a gentle Yorkshire lass, who was every bit a hapless victim as her children. What a strange world we live in. Had she herself been Jewish, she would have been highly prized within her own community, cosseted and protected, revered as the means of passing on a true kosher bloodline!

Perhaps the one positive benefit of this unfortunate alliance was that there was no requirement for the children to be brought up in the Jewish orthodox, or even liberal, tradition. My grandfather had neatly dispensed with the "faith of his fathers" after asking (probably having to beg) for financial assistance, having an ever-growing family in a time of poverty. He approached what I assume was the Jewish board of Guardians, part of the Beth Din, the council of people - for that read men - who made decisions of government and support in a particular synagogue. On this occasion, the answer was a resounding "no". The fact that he had "married out" (to a non-Jewish woman) meant that he had committed a most heinous crime, forfeiting the right to ask for help. It was a case of "don't call us", and "we won't be calling you". The Pharisees were indeed alive and well! Having shaken the dust of years (and most likely, that of the original desert) off his feet, my grandfather shed not only his past, but also his beliefs. He was between a rock and a hard place, the old, old story of conditional acceptance being told all over again.

The reluctance by one or both parents to redress the balance and to adequately handle the apparent difficulties of this Jewish/Gentile alliance and its implications left its indelible mark upon all the siblings, not least being my mother. She remembers the "secrets, whispers and being different", of being missed out of school assembly, without the slightest knowledge as to the reason why. With hindsight and a mature standpoint, it is obvious that the school thought that my mother came from a family that practiced its Jewish faith, wrongly as it happened, but with the best intentions. She had a strong memory of one particular teacher being very kind to her, the teacher, perhaps realising how confused my mother was over her identity. Having been born prematurely, my mother believed herself to be only two pounds in weight at birth. Continuing poor health and major illnesses meant that her schooling was erratic, missing much formative education and affecting her both physically and emotionally. My mother's life had been well and truly blighted by the "half and half existence", in ways that were significant, resulting in an insecurity that made it hard for her to separate from her quite large but somewhat dysfunctional family. I feel that the damage to the siblings was like the effect of a shattered mirror, distorting images and perceptions. In some ways, this couldn't fail to affect myself and my brother, him markedly so (his own sentiments).

My mother's marriage to a man whose parents seemed hostile to her on account of her background (or so she thought), only increased her loneliness. Hatred of the city she had to call home also increased with time, a lot of this being communicated to me, and making it hard for me to feel settled, and dividing my loyalties. My life became as much a game of two halves as her own life had been, a see-saw existence with me trying to put down roots in the place of my birth, loving and investing my energies in school, Sunday School Brownies and friends, only to have them snatched away at the drop of a hat, or rather the sending of a telegram or a phone call from the public phone box at our local shops (no home phones or mobiles then!). My mother, brother and I were always waiting at the coach depot for a Standerwicks coach (remember them?). Don't misunderstand me, I loved being with my grandparents, aunties and uncles as much as I loved the components of my life at home, but for different reasons. They always spent a lot of time with me, including me in their plans, taking me out on jaunts and enriching my life in all sorts of ways. My interest in reading, poetry and music was fostered, as was the playing of cards! Being a very "knowing" child and acutely aware, my "people watching" tendencies had been finely honed since my "hello man" days. I had an unfortunate knack of saying the thing you were supposed to think but should never, ever say. Well, I did! These are known in the Church of England as "the sins of commission", the doing and saying things you shouldn't. I certainly created some spectacular moments! This, at times, did not endear me to my extended family!

Part of my decision to pursue this journey into my family history was to try to restore a greater sense of pride to my mother and a better sense of wholeness than she had been allowed to feel. Previously there had only been shame, defensiveness and paranoia. This was expressed in always thinking she was regarded as an "idiot". Like a jack-in-a-box, this popped out frequently, and without warning. She wanted to be "perfect", "to belong", but not wanting "to join." Her collective family life had resulted in tensions and schisms that seemed to have had complex and root causes other than the usual sibling rivalries, some seemingly irreparable, the same patterns arising over and over. Perhaps the injection of foreign temperament accounted for it. What is sad is the almost complete lack of curiosity they displayed about the "soil" out of which they had been "grown", or any awareness of the sheer cost and bravery of that which their grandparents had undertaken. This is possibly no different from a lot of other families, but I just want it to be! None of them ever knew their grandfather, Abraham, never questioned his absence. and weren't aware he had actually died. They never knew that he had been buried in a Jewish cemetery in Leeds, fairly nearby to their grandmother's home. They had therefore, never visited the grave, nor left a stone on it, as befits Jewish custom, denoting the last person to have visited. This very biblical symbolic action is the equivalent of a "calling card". It wouldn't be at all surprising that the life Abraham had led had contributed to his death at just sixty years of age. I think he may have been made to serve for several years in the Russian army, the Tsar making this compulsory for all Jewish young men, subjecting them to as much hardship and cruelty as possible. In addition, the Tsar stripped the Jews of their trade and skill, demoting them to undignified positions of lowliness and rendering them only as artisans rather artists in their own right. Obviously, the aims were to demoralise them and ensure the denial of earning power. If they managed to escape being killed, they could apply for transportation by ship to Europe. Someone was supposed to stand as guarantor for the passage, some I expect, not exactly waiting for this "official" route to freedom! I would have thought that it all took a toll on his health, leading to his early death.

Annie, their grandmother, fared better in that she lived a much longer life .Her granddaughters were taken quite frequently by my grandma, her daughter-in-law, to visit her in her little back-to-back house in the sprawling Yorkshire city. My grandma apparently warned her daughters against eating the gefilte fish, cooked on the open fire. Then again, my grandma was the expert in warning people off things that were exciting. Had it been me, she would have used her "oldie but goldie" phrase, "she's highly strung, you know. She mustn't" - do whatever it was I wasn't supposed to do. In resurrecting that from the back of my mind, it leaves me feeling like I was some sort of human tennis racket! Anyway, that was Grandma, who seemed to think of me as another one of her daughters, tacked onto the end of the gaggle of girls and who, together with the two boys, made up this band of not always happy pilgrims. In fact, a kind of collective mentality existed, often prevalent in large families, and possibly more so between females. When something happens to one, it transmits itself to the others, becoming a real "sheep-thing". It's almost on a par with the connection between twins, with or without the "sixth" sense aspect.

So, that's my background, the soil from which I grew. Like the classic sign of a stroke, my Jewishness is only down one side and then only half of that, the equivalent of a head and arm or maybe a leg. However, this does nothing to diminish the fascination with the bloodline, and the desire to be associated with that stiff necked, proud, suffering yet resilient race amongst whom God actually chose to place His Son for reasons only known by Him. This, together with the more romantic and exotic aspects of Belarus or "Beautiful Russia", act like a boomerang where the whole thing keeps coming back! Like many, many people, I am making a valiant attempt to research my family's history. There seems to be an imperative for me to find the little Russian town of my great grandparents' birth. Along with Zoe Wanamaker, David Suchet, David Baddiel, Steven Fry, Natasha Kaplinsky and other third generation Jews whose origins were in

Eastern Europe, I too want to make that connection with my distant past. I share that "need to know" desire to fill in the branch which helps complete my family tree, looking backwards in order to go forward. It may be that in trying to know my forbears, I will understand myself more and will recognise traits of my character that have up until now have remained a mystery. I have certainly experienced a fair amount of being the family scapegoat, particularly by the second and third generations - a very Old Testament concept but slightly out of step, it being the third and fourth generations that had trouble visited on them! It was observed by one in-law as guilt by association, a sort of "kick the cat" mentality. Was this yet another genetic imprint? I know that I possess a steely determination to get from A to B by looking straight down the middle of a situation and assessing the circumstances quickly in order to hatch a plan - most of the time, that is! Self-belief, plus the desire to stay alive must have carried my great grandparents through the most frightening and gruelling time of their lives. Sometimes, when I am really tired, I start to lose touch with who I am, but I expect they couldn't afford to do that in their determination to create a new life. My great grandparents were religious Jews, and being people of prayer, I wonder if they prayed for those who would follow in their footsteps? I wonder if those in the family who currently embrace faith are the result of their faithful prayers? Am I part of that prayer? As a descendant of not only my great-grandfather Abraham, but also of Abraham, the Father of All Nations, the answer has to be "Yes"!

Paul Simon, my songwriter and word-smith hero, is a descendant of Eastern European immigrants, described in one of his songs as "the third generation of the boat". He is the tip of a creative iceberg, a countless raft of sophisticated and urbane musicians, dancers, cabaret artists, actors and other creative avenues. Where would we have been without George Gershwin, Irving Berlin, Al Jolson and countless others of the Tin Pan Alley days? Artistic life and expression would have been the poorer without Leonard Bernstein, Barbara Streisand, Andre Previn and the like. You only have to listen to Bob Dylan's gritty take on life or Paul Simon's carefully crafted lyrics to discover how his Eastern European Jewish roots are still significant in the shaping and underpinning of his life. His line "One and one half wandering Jew" refers to his previous wife, Star Wars actress Carrie Fisher, the daughter of actor Eddie Fisher and actress Debbie Reynolds. Like him or loathe him, Barry "Copacobana" Manilow is another highly successful songster with a great line in schmaltz, adored by housewives and star struck young girls the world over. As a young boy, his golden voice wooed the worshippers at his local synagogue. He's since wowed women the world over! Britain has had its fair share of Jewish talent too. Its famous Jewish sons and daughters include Frankie Vaughan, Mike and Bernie Winters, Helen Shapiro, disc jockey David Jacobs, Jimmy Tarbuck, recognisable names spearheading the acres of others in the firmament. The "poor boy made good" syndrome has not been the total preserve of the song and dance people. The ability possessed by Jews to make money and to succeed is acknowledged by one and all, whether in the spheres of diamonds, sport, entertainment, commerce, and even crime! A prime example of this can be found in London barrow boy, Jack Cohen, who used his humble beginnings to seize his opportunity to build one of today's gigantic and successful enterprises, that ubiquitous household name, Tesco. His entrepreneurial skills were the basis of today's phenomenal empire. My husband even met him when he worked as a computer operator for the burgeoning business many years ago, the computers in those days still being the size of a small city!

This is just a thumbnail sketch of the harvest reaped from the influx of resourceful, determined people and their descendants, the Jewish Diaspora scattering its people all over the world. They are now being gathered and repatriated once more to Israel, the land of their Fathers. This re-grouping of the modern day tribes means that it is once more a nation in its own right - admittedly, a troubled and troubling nation, disparate and diverse in Jewish flavour but nevertheless a nation. Spiritually, however is has forfeited the right to its own title deeds - for the time being - with its insistence that its Messiah has yet to appear - for the first time! Even Paul Simon has astutely observed, "If the answer is infinite light, why do we sleep in the dark?" As for our genes, and regardless of our race, we are all a product of two halves, two streams of blood joined together to form one river, providing us with two lots of everything - okay when there is an equable outcome but not when there is genetic overloading, causing an avalanche of destruction. As regards my own bloodline, the Jewish effect is a bit like diluted Ribena! It may look pale but the taste is distinctive! So, in looking at the "third generation of the boat" (and off it), I have to include myself. In doing so, it answers why I feel the need to search and align and maybe the need to "prove". The almost comically lugubrious rabbi of our local synagogue, all hand gestures and the weariness of the world upon his Lithuanian shoulders said to me, "Why?" My answer then was "Because" - a bit existentialist at the time, maybe, but that was before my programme of excavation had possessed me! Perhaps it's a bit like carrying the Olympic flag - a case of "it's my moment", my turn to remind the world that my antecedents had been here. Perhaps I am simply here for such a time as this, "wearing my father's old coat" as the song suggests, or in my case, that of my great-grandfather's.

At the time of writing, America had just achieved her impossible dream: they had voted in the first black President of the United States, finally achieving her goal as Land of the Free and Home of the Brave. In so doing, it has flung its metaphorical prison doors wide open, hopefully liberating and restoring the spirit not only of those of black origin but the spirit of Man everywhere. This surely has to exceed the "one small step for man, one giant step for mankind" moon landing! President Barack Obama, (black but not entirely so), eloquent, highly educated, charismatic and like so many past American presidents, a man of Christian conviction, has carried in his gene pool the struggles and identity of his forbears. He fulfilled a promise to redeem the past by achieving and securing a foothold and pathway for the future and for all whom he represents, much like Abraham for the future of Israel. For the untold many in the world, he has made the words of the old hymn live - "through many dangers, toils and snares we have already come... and grace shall lead us home". In achieving such, he has redressed the balance for the world, past and present, the Rowland's Hut of equality, justice and acceptance. So, I think we can raise our glasses, and in our own time honoured ways say, "Cheers", "Here's looking at you, Baby", and for all my kinsfolk, "Locheim"!

Having looked back, I can now continue my walk down "The Long and Winding Road" of my journey, an all-time favourite Paul McCartney song and sentiment. Armed with just a bit more insight into the "where, when and who" questions we all need answering, it is clear that the "why" is not a fact but a feeling. It is a long echo from somewhere in time and space, a deeply felt call travelling through the genes, joining the ancient past to the present. I came across the following passage in The Message version of the Bible which describes the blessing Joseph bestowed upon his grandchildren:-

"The God before whom walked my fathers Abraham and Isaac, The god who has been my shepherd all my life long to this very day, The Angel who delivered me from every evil, Bless the boys. May my name be echoed in their lives, and the names of Abraham and Isaac, my fathers, and may they grow covering the earth with their children." This goes a long way in reinforcing what I have been feeling, that journey to the centre of myself, where past and present meet.

In journeying there, I have discovered greater significance in the events of the biblical journey. In re-enacting the Pesach, Pasach or to us, the Passover at my church, I felt a sense of awe in having experienced that which my long family line had practiced as part and parcel of their lives. Added to this is the recent realization that I would not have existed were it not for someone painting the door-frame with blood on the night before the Exodus from Egypt. This is a wondrous thought! Once again, there was God's acknowledgement that the home and its occupants was a sanctuary, a place of safety under Him. There goes that Hut again! By beginning with Rowland's Hut, I have been able to travel "back to the future" to discover the binding thread that has kept Mankind stitched together, the place where safety, acceptance, belonging and the importance of being fulfilled can be exercised so that a person can develop a secure, whole, and grounded centre. Home is the place where we first experience this idea of a haven, a shelter from the storm. It's the place where we can take our first faltering steps in relating to others, the place where we can take our bruised souls as well as our grazed knees! If experienced positively, it becomes the model of how to belong and how to recover, providing a blueprint of how to feel secure. It is a biblical model, showing us the way God ideally wants us to be. He knew a thing or two about connection, the Bible speaking about how "He sets the lonely in families. It was the family God created, the family God preserved at times of biblical crisis for the furtherance of the human race. It was for the furtherance of my family that my great grandparents left what was very possibly their chicken shed home of security (inside, if not outside its walls), making their life changing but life saving journey, and it was for the Christian family that Rowland offered his Hut. I have heard that the house in whose grounds the Hut stood is still standing, escaping the recent housing developments surrounding it. The Hut is possibly no longer there, but that does nothing to diminish the memories and the impact it made.

I hope that my words have done justice to those deserving it - to Abraham and Annie, those "Wandering Jews", to my mother and her immediate family members and, of course, to Rowland who, by offering us his hut for our togetherness became the provider of the theme that inspired me. A home, a hut, a house or a chicken shed "speak" the same language, saying, "we belong, we give love and care, we accept you, we will look after you and nurture you." They are places for dreams, for togetherness, for significance. They are reflections of God's House, the place to bring our battered selves, to find refuge, and to seek sanctuary so that we can be turned round, dusted down and sent out refreshed, inspired and once more ready to cope. This has to happen before we can find our purpose and give of our best. Whether in nineteenth century Russia or the global twenty first century with its uncertainties and economic downturn, we can initiate a search. We can search to find a place where we can feel held in the arms of God, loved by His Son and each other made alive in the Person of His Spirit. That can be an extremely tall order, but we have to try so that we can taste what is to come, that Rowland's Hut of all time, our Eternal Home!

At the end of every episode of my all-time favourite childhood programme, "The Flowerpot Men", someone always spoke the words, "and I think the little house knew something about it, don't you?". In the light of events, I do, I most definitely do!

Chapter 2: Who'd Like To Be In America?

"Not I, said the fly, with my little eye."
- with apologies to no-one in particular!

I was eleven years old and was reaching one of life's crossroad moments - I was about to leave the school that had become my second womb. With the Eleven Plus exam behind me, (there goes that pantomime moment again!) and my academic fate signed, sealed and delivered, I was enjoying the last golden weeks of my primary school childhood. Our class of "Fifty Nine" was looking forward to the "away week" trip, the preserve and reward for being nudged out of the primary school nest. The collective temperature of our top junior class was steadily rising and threatening to erupt into a storm. Then it happened, not a literal storm, but a thunderbolt that was to alter my whole summer and the years that followed, together with my view and perception of certain events and places. Instead of the final bonding exercise with my classmates of the last few years and travelling with them by train to a destination in the south of England, I would be boarding an ocean going liner which was none other than The Queen Mary! I was being taken on a life - enhancing trip to the United States of America, where I would be staying for three months at the home of my mother's older sister. She had gone to America as a classic G.I. Bride, having met and married her soldier husband in England in the Forties.

The end of May signalled the end of an era. My premature departure from school meant that I was leaving behind the routines and patterns of the last six or so years. There was the security of the reception class at five years old, with pastel drawings on the board of umbrellas, balls and the like. There was school assembly, with its marching in and out, and its familiar hymns and prayers. There was morning milk and playtimes, which were spent in doing my knitting, playing "cat's cradle" on the wall with my friends or walking round the quadrangle to the classrooms doing a job as a monitor, all happy, rainbow-minded memories. The fact that I was leaving before everyone else in my year emphasized the wrench in my soul, but leaving I was! With all my Goodbyes behind me, and my new and shiny holiday clothes packed and ready, the day of departure dawned, a grey day, a grey Southampton dock and a huge ship in seemingly grey water. It was not the most prepossessing of starts. However, this was about to give way to three sun drenched months, progressive heat and sudden, spectacular storms - in more ways than one, prophetically speaking. The embarkation and departure were just like all those you may have seen in old films, the passengers hanging over the sides of the vessel, waving and being waved at, the huge funnels sounding their horns as the Grand Old Dame inched out of the moorings and the increasingly dot-like people on the dock side gradually disappearing. My dad disappeared from view as well, only to come back into it at the end of August.

Meanwhile, there was the legendary glamour of the famous ship to discover, with its impressive sweeping staircases, formally presented dining rooms (I don't remember a captain or his table, but there must have been one!), mahogany clad lounges and a swimming pool whose water swished and swayed with increasing impact, the more mid-Atlantic we became. The endlessly long, windswept decks with rows of chairs (for the hardy!) and the challenge of its deck quoits games, provided a welcome breather for passengers who needed a break from the luxury inside. The standard sleeping cabins were not quite the calibre of above stairs. It seemed as if we were in the bowels of the earth, with strange shuddering and rumblings, presumably from the engines, endlessly present as I tried to sleep. However, the whole thing was so surreal as to provide a welcome respite from the "wake up to reality" time to follow. The knowledge that the then Sir Anthony Wedgewood Benn and family were fellow travellers (first class, of course!) created a frisson of excitement to on-board life. Me being me, I had taken myself off on a Mission to see if I could get myself through the barrier - yes folks, an actual barrier, behind which the numerous Wedgewood Benn members were secreted. The system did not allow the likes of me to penetrate the Holy of voyaging Holies, and I never did glimpse this living legend or his family. Our names appear on the same passenger list - different categories of course. Prior to him downgrading to plain old Tony, Sir Anthony was still a bit of a Big Benn in those days!

Standing on the deck of this monster sailing ship, and surveying a New York early morning, was something of a culture shock. Unbeknown to me, we had sailed past that bastion of America's freedom, the Statue of Liberty and had docked overnight. With skyscrapers towering over the ship to both port and starboard (note how nautical I'd become!) and the sounds of the day revving up all around, it was time to disembark and to be decanted into the awaiting heat and frenetic madness of the Big Apple. We looked for its core, but it was more a case of "cor!" and "I'm an eleven year old - get me out of here!" There was a palpable sense of danger in the air, made worse by the skyscrapers pressing down from their lofty heights and casting shadows on the criss-crossing streets. Manic taxi drivers stopped their vehicles at the drop of a hat and went head- to- head with the nearest victim, all gestures and expletives. The driving was on a par with the Parisians circling the Arc de Triomphe with an "every man for himself" policy. At some point in this American day, we began our long journey to Detroit, Michigan, travelling overland, and overnight, in what was optimistically called a Greyhound Bus. Already disoriented from the days at sea, we undertook a trip through what seemed like a million, trillion States of America - yes, I do know there aren't that many but I was now in somewhat of an altered state myself, the biggest "state" being me! We passed through Pennsylvania and Philadelphia, Pittsburgh and Harrisburg (a one horse town and not entirely sure about the one-trick pony!). It was only marginally better than Orange in France where I needed squatter's rights to go to what was laughingly called a toilet - a hole in the floor! After twenty something hours in a tin container, the sum total of my knowledge of things American passed by on the other side. I know just how the victim in the Good Samaritan story felt.

It was around this time that my head, throbbing and shuddering, began to feel like the size of the Empire State building that we'd left behind several dislocated hours ago. Or maybe it was more like a rocket getting ready for lift-off at Cape Canaveral. Either way, my head knew it had arrived on the other side of the Pond, feeling as if it didn't have room to fit. Or was I about to have one - a fit, that is? It so happened that I was spared the trouble, as a man on the return journey (three months down the line) conveniently had one for me. I say convenient - I was lying! As the bus bowled along, Greyhound- style, it followed the shoreline of Lake Huron. Lulled into a travelling stupor, I was rudely jerked back to reality by the man's almighty writhing seizure. I remember wondering who was going to win, the bus or the man. The whole episode took on the character of a Hieronymous Bosch painting, not being sure where destruction was next going to strike. When it all finally subsided and we reached a stopping point, I nearly fell out of the dubious dog-named vehicle and kissed the ground. We had actually arrived at Niagara Falls for a one-night stop over. It was a real "By the time I get to Phoenix" moment! I have to admit that at this juncture I felt very much like Derek, our folk music associate who maintains, "When you've seen one hill you've seen them all". For hill, substitute falls! I stood looking over the Niagara phenomenon feeling completely under-whelmed. Had it been today, I would have been very Catherine Tate, muttering "whatever".

They weren't the only things to fall. Our faces performed a passable imitation when we met the fleas and cockroaches that were sharing our accommodation! They didn't exactly make us feel welcome and clearly hadn't attended the "Have a nice day" training school of America. Still, as my deputy head intoned (often, it must be said) "Per ardua ad astra". It seemed more like an advancing asteroid than upward to the stars, twinkling or otherwise! What with the Fit Man, the nightmare scenario that transpired and the unappetising thought of our room mates, I felt I was back in primary school prayers, reciting "for ever and ever and ever…. and ever and ever", without the Amen which should have brought all things to a close! It may have been more appropriate, in time honoured fashion by those feeling desperate, to have rolled over the Falls in a barrel! At this point, something reminded me of the fact that I was English, damn you and must at all costs get back to the Motherland - and if Mothercare had existed, then I would have gone there too, not being too sure of either Mother or Land. You know how it is - any port in a storm? Or was it storm in a port? Either way, I had obviously spent too much time at sea!

Anyway, I will rewind this rather sorry tale to my arrival, which strangely enough, came before my departure from the Land of the Free and Home of the brave. In view of the following proceedings, freedom and bravery were to take on a whole new dimension. I liken it to what I will call the "baby birds in the nest" syndrome where, because of jealousy, sibling rivalry, hunger or just plain overcrowding (oh yes, that covers it admirably!), some birds decide to snack on other more vulnerable birds. It's as though the mother bird leaves a note stating, "I'll be gone some time. If necessary, eat your brother or sister". Now this more or less sums up the situation. Take two, sisters that is, one largely absent husband on account of working permanent nights and a matriarchal mother. Add to this several assorted minors - a miniature prima donna, one educationally challenged and one female who was reading, marking, learning and inwardly digesting everything but food ("it's too hot to feed you"). Yes - you've guessed the identity of that one! The ensemble was completed by a seemingly unaware young male (well, aren't they always?) but mostly unaware of the gathering storm clouds that I, in the role of Mini not-very Ha Ha could see on the horizon.

On returning from a trip out in a neighbour's car one afternoon, the sad prophecy had materialized. There, on the lawn for all to see, was the sum total of our possessions, the whole kitbag, kit and caboodle, tarnished with the shame of exposure. The street needed to know that "Someone" had committed a heinous crime, the punishment being a very public expulsion - ours! How I wished for that soaring American eagle to carry me far away so that my heart, trying to force its way out of my chest could slow down and reverse the body shock. I was eleven years old and in a strange land that was growing steadily stranger by the minute. The sun seemed to go down, my blood ran cold and despite the August heat, I was fast turning into a block of ice. "Where would we go? What would we do, and who would we do it with?" My mother's mind seemed absent without leave, and my dad was three thousand deep, wet miles away. Did he even know about this shocking turn of events? Did he know that this American Dream had faded?

I have never been given to those "Somewhere over the rainbow" moments, but this was one time when the land of Judy Garland's song was suddenly very appealing. However, kindly neighbours came to our rescue. On hearing of our plight, we were divided up between two homes and looked after until our day of departure. I, of course, had to be a "BIG GIRL", being the eldest, so was separated from my erstwhile and distracted mother and my younger brother. It wasn't all bad, providing you didn't mind being driven around by the family's fourteen year old daughter (fourteen?) to Top Hat or White Castle, the Nineteen Fifties' equivalent of McDonalds establishments. At least I could resume eating more regularly again! I realise with hindsight, that marvellous "after the event" gift, God had erected a soft and very reassuring Rowland's Hut over our predicament, where we could lick our wounds and gather strength in order to make what was to prove our difficult and tricky return journey. It is unthinkable that anyone, let alone family, could act so inhumanely but "there's nowt so queer as folk"! So, fast-forward again to the Fit-man, Lake Huron, dodgy buses and flea-pit flop-houses. Perhaps there's a certain Jack Kerouac charm to all of this? I wasn't aware at the time of either the writer or any charm in the situation. I was, however, aware of the desperate need to get going and to get back to all that was familiar and to leave the tarnished experience of this "tinsel town" country well and truly behind. As they say, "boy oh boy! Just a cotton pickin' minute, but what about girl oh girl?"

So, we were back in New York, walking on the wild side and comparing yet another Hotel de Flea-pit that was our hotel with the chic opulence of Macy's and Gimble's, the retail paradises of the time. Personally, I would have given anything for a whiff of Woolworth's. Yes, I know they had the Dime store and the Five and Ten Cent, all amounting to the same thing but it really wasn't the same at all! At the time of writing, Woolies is now very sadly no more. You only really had a deep appreciation of your local store on your return from foreign shores, together with a cup - no, an urn of tea, proper tannin-loaded tea. I felt much the same about needing a pork chop on a return from France, instead of the leg of horse that had been passed off as something de manger! Most people I know have had a real longing to be in New York, whereas I just saw it as a holding operation, waiting for the "all aboard the good ship lollipop" signal. The skyscrapers, the United Nations Building, and the whole of the fashionable and cosmopolitan society on the move hardly registered on my Richter scale of interest. There were the contrasting poor areas around the docks, where every sloping and steamy street appeared to end in a huge ocean-going liner, the famous names of which I had seen advertised in travel brochures. Each seemed almost casually tied up in fathoms of dark, endless water, totally accessible and scarily beckoning to the onlooker, but definitely not this onlooker! I, who went wobbly on the edge of the local model boating lake, was not about to test my survival instincts!

On finally boarding what was the palatial Queen Elizabeth the First liner for the homeward journey, I remained resolutely unrepentant in my appreciation of my surroundings - just deeply relieved to be on my way. My vast disappointment over the recent debacle contributed to my feelings boiling over in a final rage (well deserved in my estimation). The catalyst for this outburst was the waiter allotted to serving the lunchtime meal in the posh dining room after boarding the ship and leaving New York. On finally sitting down to the first decent meal for days, I wanted soup - not an unreasonable request, you would have thought. I was actually refused (in Brooklynese if you please) with a "If oy give your little goyl soup in this heat, she'll doy". It's a wonder he didn't "doy", that is at "moy" hands and with his "foyce" in the soup I didn't get given. I am well aware that my use of English has suddenly deteriorated but so had I, deteriorated in all things English, that is! I didn't need a stranger telling me the state of my digestive system, after having spent three months on that well-known "hamburgers alternating with starvation" diet! I was with Tom Jones on this one, just wanting the "green, green grass of home" and possibly the sheep that grazed on it. I craved meat and two veg – two, five, ten - I didn't care! Throw in stodgy puds, beans on toast and school dinners. You name it and I would have eaten it, including the waiter's hand!

It's probably best to draw a veil over the impossibility of having to share sleeping arrangements with your Grandma when there was a cold war in place. However, even that became "normal" in the scheme of things. As long as this was the only iceberg I was going to encounter on the journey (my geographic knowledge temporarily deserting me), I would be able to manage the remaining few days with a "so what's new" policy. The days passed, the billows rolled and gradually, the American Dream faded (more nightmare in my case) and the weather and on-board culture took a decidedly more British turn. The Mid-Atlantic rock and roll motion caused the fading American tans to turn to green- that's if the owners of the faces were not already lying prone in their rock and rolling cabins. I became the only one in the swimming pool, the only one prowling round and round the windswept decks where I became obsessive in checking and counting the lifeboats - chained, cradled and positioned in serried ranks. A small but worrying inner voice alerted me to the reality of there not actually being enough for everyone - should that "Titanic" moment ever occur. I managed to muffle it sufficiently, diverting my attention towards the next meal. I was now allowed to make my own choices, given that we were once more in cooler (much, much cooler!) climes. It certainly was an apt case of "if you can't stand the heat, get out of the kitchen." The eminently collectable menus, nostalgically illustrated with views of English beauty spots and places of interest such as Wookey Hole in Somerset and Stonehenge, helped a great deal in readjusting. Everything was shrinking to recognisable size again after the conditioning of the past few months. So, collect them I did, along with the complimentary postcards featuring the ship and other souvenirs of the luxury vessel, these being widely available in the public lounges and libraries. I still have some of them today, along with the aforesaid passenger lists. These were collectable, if only for the listed celebrities. Perhaps these were the forerunners of OK and HELLO MAGAZINES, yesterday's politicians being today's Wags and Wannabes!

It was with the greatest thankfulness and possibly in a state of near insanity that I finally sailed into port. What was I expecting to see? Was it the scene of Basil Fawlty's feverish imagination - the herds of wildebeests, sweeping majestically over the plains of

Torquay? I must say that he and I almost had a meeting of minds, and it wouldn't have taken much to end up with him on Planet Loony. No, what I saw was just Good Old Blighty - and I wasn't even born until after the War! If there had been Union Jacks (none of this Union Flag lark!), I would have wrapped myself up in them like the Olympic runners on their laps of honour. I was back in the Land of my Fathers - but not necessarily the Land of my Great and Great, Great Grandfathers. As soon as the gangplank was lowered (eye patch and stripy jumper in place, me hearties) I was off that Q.E. The First like the proverbial bat and back into the bosom of our grey, gloomy, small, slightly grubby but oh so familiar patch of land that is forever England. There was a band playing, in my head if not in real life, and its tune was the one speaking of our hope and glory. It was First Night, Middle Night, Last Night and Every Night of the Proms as far as I was concerned. I was back on terra English firma with its small buildings, cars, shops and people- oh yes, definitely much smaller people! Like the description of the numerous homes dotted around, I had "Dun Roamin" for the time being. Even being put in my place by my father for being my usual lippy self with a "that's enough" glare (specially invented by parents of Post-War children) I knew I was Home, back in my place and, once again, comfortable in my skin - well, relatively speaking, given I had been in baking sun and often un-air-conditioned heat for weeks. I'm tempted, like Wallace to say "that were a grand day out, Gromit", but in all fairness, I would have to substitute Vomit for Gromit!

I only had a brief few days in this blissful state before my next momentous challenge rose to hit me between the eyes - that of Secondary School. No sooner had I said Bye, Bye Miss American Pie than it was time to exchange pedal pushers (American long shorts, if you see what I mean) for gym-slips and blazers, satchels, set squares and compasses. The latter seemed as sinister as the hypodermic needle used to inject me with some protective substance before my encounter with the States. It was also effective in making me fall to the floor in a dead faint after merely glimpsing it! By the way, just what was a set-square? If travel was supposed to broaden the mind, it hadn't done much for my mathematical ability! In contrast to the cosy and familiar surroundings of the primary school that had been my world, the new school had seemed a daunting and alien prospect. However, after the last three months, it didn't seem a problem any more. What had appeared as huge and unconquerable had shrunk to a mere pleasant and purpose built establishment with landscaped grounds, a pond (quite a lot smaller than the one I'd crossed a few days ago!) and a new swimming pool. Was it really only last week? My, how the Eagle had flown – but how the sparrow had landed!

It was Autumn, or as they say State-side, The Fall. Everything family-wise had certainly done that! However, time and tide wait for no man and as normal a service as possible had been resumed, quieter but resumed. After the trauma of the summer, the dust had settled and the rhythm of life had been restored. A new fridge had been installed at home (very American!), but more importantly, my new school was utterly absorbing. I had new friends, new subjects (some of them potentially worrying) and new classmates to compete with in my two favourite subjects, music and English. The best thing of all was my brilliant housemistress whose role allowed her to create a wonderful, warm and generous Rowland's Hut over us all. I, for one, will remain eternally grateful to her for providing fun, interest, enthusiasm and fair discipline. Her own subject was music (Hooray!), the biggest plus in my book! I expect we were the usual cheeky bunch of eleven year olds, but she allowed us to be ourselves as far as was possible whilst encouraging our musical interests. It helped that we were in a completely new building and we were the first occupants. Everything was provided for - shiny lockers for books, special racks for coats and sports equipment, a house-room for communal activities and the brand new toilets where adolescent girls crooned the latest Cliff Richard song, "Living Doll" into the mirrors, back-combing their hair at the same time!

After a time that hadn't exactly been the Summer of Love, I embraced this new phase of my life with renewed energy and interest. I wore my uniform and its status with pride, learned the ropes of being a "Big Girl" in a more diverse setting than primary school had offered and generally found enough content on which to focus. Another plus was the approaching Christmas – the Silent Night season. In the extended family context, there were many of those but there was also a sense that everything was Calm and Bright too. Besides, my other Grandma and Grandad lived nearby and supplied what Grandparents supply. Despite my smooth transition into new school life, the seat of anxiety marked "vacant" was soon filled. I developed allergies towards algebra, geometry, slippery set-squares and unruly compasses. My cup was full and running over but not necessarily all drinkable. My nervous system was, at times, taken over by an enemy. An E.C.G. reading would possibly have worried anyone concerned with affairs of the heart! Every maths lesson seemed like it was a gangster holding a gun to my head, only blotted out by doing my music homework- disloyal, I know but better than the Prozac we didn't have access to in those days.

So, from the angle of my dislike of certain subjects, my school year developed into a kind of football game, the two teams being English and music versus everything else. Occasionally divinity, biology and art would beef up the score but physics, chemistry and Bunsen burners would threaten relegation. My utter relief at being declared incapable of G.C.E. in the latter subjects overcame any sense of pride, wounded or otherwise. The thought of being taught by the equivalent of a female crocodile in a pink nylon overall, a gash of red lipstick making her mouth look like a pillar-box, did nothing to tempt me near a laboratory, her natural habitat. Together with her red pen, she was always ready to express her disgust at my feeble grasp of all things H2O. Yes Siree, I could be as incapable as necessary and for as long as it took! This would leave me free to pursue my happy relationship with words and music. I relished every English essay, music lesson, choir practice, music competition and concert. The end of term house entertainment was never a problem. I'd whip up a little something and away we'd all go - not with the "name, age, sex - occasionally" precocity of the fourth years but with that ever so earnest, slightly cheeky offering of the first and second year variety, leaving us flushed with pride and clapped out - in both senses of the word!

The year was winding its way toward the end of year exams. Looming much larger were my tonsils, which decided to put me through another spectacularly hideous patch, resulting in an appointment at the hospital with the Ear, Nose and Throat Man. Sounding like a song and dance act, one certainly was performed between said man and my mother. The broken English of the Polish consultant clashed with the unbroken temperament of my Half-Chosen-Race mother who, upon questioning the need for surgery managed to get me struck off the list and flung out of his presence, possibly accompanied by his spitting on his palms, book, and maybe the floor, which I wished would swallow me up! I can imagine the crowd outside were yelling "once more with feeling!". In retrospect, I could have given it my best shot with the following ditty, sung to the tune of "Oh Mr Porter, what shall I do?". Anyway, in the best pantomime tradition, here s your chance to sing along, with a one, two, three, four - "Oh Dr. Kander, What shall I do? My tonsils are doing a war dance and I don t know what to do. Get your knife of choice out, as quickly as you can. Oh Dr. Kander, what a poorly girl I am!" There followed the most tonsibilis horribilis of a time. From the summer to the autumn, I alternated between the living and the nearly dead (or so it felt) and knew that I could kiss goodbye to any chance of making it into the newly inaugurated school inter-house singing competition, to be held in the spring term. I was in no position to be "inter" anything! I was now in possession of streptococcal throat, a condition that rendered me mainly lifeless for most of each day.

It was a seemingly innocent and life sapping morning, identical with all other recent mornings. School was a distant memory as I lay in my parlous state on the sofa, watching the test card on telly. Well, that was as close as you got to morning television! Actually, sometimes there would be what I suppose was the forerunner of a documentary on Mozart. The accompanying music was the glorious Eine Kleine Nachtmusik, which was thrilling and helped diminish the burning pit that had become my throat. I gradually became aware of a timorous knocking on the front door, accompanying the knocking on my throat. Upon answering this (the door, not my throat) I entered a surreal, topsy-turvy world of the emotions as I discovered my Grandma, fresh from her year of estrangement, weeping and wailing all over our doorstep.

Apparently, there was some drama over my mother's sister, also estranged but obviously about to be used as a tool of reconciliation and re-union. It obviously wasn't enough to have our own quota of grief - our doorstep was now soaked with someone else's! After all, wasn't I waiting to be re-instated on the Master Surgeon's (or should that be Butcher's?) operating list? It is this point that the director of a film shouts, "cut", applicable on all levels really but on my tonsils, most definitely. However, it was not Cecil B. De Mille conducting this particular drama but my Grandma. I did my twelve-year-old level best as Peace Envoy in the absence of - well, everyone else in the household! Had they known something I didn't?

That was the end of the Stand Off, and with it came the drip, drip, drip of a slow thaw. Progress was cautious with new but mainly temporary boundaries in place. Any visits to my maternal grandparents ensured a stay in a nice (sorry, Mr Tucker, for that word that you found abhorrent and banned from our junior school essays!) hotel, the departure from a lifetime's habit seeming exciting and cavalier. As the schism narrowed, it wasn't long before we were back in the bosom (and beds) of the family. I expect the adults were all on their best behaviour but I can't vouch for my tendency to be liberal with my opinions! Maybe my condition kept me in check. If not, there was always THAT LOOK that my Dad had perfected!

About the same time that the family "skin graft" was under way, it was finally agreed by the hospital that I was now a suitable case for treatment, as they say. In view of what had taken place the year before, I could have told them that! Dr. Kander had relented (I wonder if he reversed the palms, book and floor spitting?). My tonsils were going to be uprooted, together with some related appendage called adenoids. Out they came, along with those of a fellow victim. Having been housed on an adult female ward, the nature of which was a mystery to our thirteen-year-old minds, our main aim was to avoid the eyes of any nurse bearing syringes, in case she bore down on us with her unwelcome injections! After our operations, we apparently provided the "in-house" entertainment as we noisily and verbally came round from the anaesthetic! Enduring aspirin gargles, tepid ice cream, unintelligible adult conversation and Shirley Bassey belting out "As long as he needs me" on the ward radio, I recovered enough to totter home where I slept for the best part of a week. Once my throat had stopped feeling like it had been rubbed with sandpaper, I started to enjoy my new tonsil free existence, not to mention my adenoids!

Within six weeks, I was back in full verbal and vocal swing, entering and winning the coveted senior solo prize in the competition I'd thought I'd never see! The adjudicator remarked she'd never heard anyone so young with such a vibrato. Funny - I wonder if Dr. Kander had put a bit in (vibrato, that is) when he performed my tonsillectomy? Or had the removal of my adenoids clinched it? Either way, it was the Rowland's Hut of all rewards for the rotten years I'd been through - a kind of "rotten roll"? It was, after all, the era of Elvis Presley, the "rotten roll" King! Having spent most of my young life in a state of tonsil hell, it was exhilarating to have left it all behind. The competition provided one of the few "I've won" moments in my life, leaving me wondering whether I should have asked if the right decision had been made. Talk about God moving in mysterious ways! I'm sure He had engineered the whole thing and feel certain He'd got me in His view, perhaps closer. This seemed to be a watershed in other ways as well. It was around this time that I was invited to go to something called the Girl Crusaders. Did I go? Of course I did — and the rest, as they say, is History!

Chapter 3: Here Come The Girls

With no apologies to that well known chain of chemists!

In the beginning was the word (with a small w!) and not exactly on the streets, more a word of mouth thing, a personal invite in your ear. Now, the word was Crusaders or to be pedantic, The Girl Crusaders. If we are going to be precise, the full title was The Girl Crusaders Union. Now, I can already hear the cogs whirring in your heads! The answer, my friends, is not blowing in the wind but rather in the explanation that the G.C.U. was a Christian evangelical organization which sought to nurture and guide young females into developing a personal relationship with God the Father, Son and Holy Spirit. Was there a male equivalent? Of course! There was also a step too far (for some!) in the form of mixed groups, but regrettably not in our neck of the woods. You will need to bear in mind that I'm talking about the early nineteen sixties when life amongst young (and certainly young Christian) people was still being guarded and chaperoned by our self appointed custodians of morality.

Regardless of its limitations, it was a watershed, a time when we swished and swayed our way through the storms of adolescence and into our late teens, some spectacular pyrotechnics being displayed along the way! It was also a time that we, like snakes, involuntarily shed the skins of childhood, exchanging them for ones that seemed initially ill-fitting, their new markings as yet unfamiliar. I suppose these skins were enabling us to explore a new territory, as yet undiscovered. However, each person's metamorphosis did not hamper us in forming a strong and highly significant friendship group, one that held most, if not all things in common - schooldays, music, some playing piano and other instruments, choir, Christian Union, weekend socializing (when eating, talking and even bitching could be served on the menu, the latter emphasized by Linda's mum serving thick cream with our coffee and calling us little cats!). I'm fully aware that my metaphors have been well and truly mixed - dogs, cats, and so early in this literary affair!

There was carol singing for charity, Crusader holiday camps, the odd party (boys?) and Away Days, often to hear the latest hot evangelical speaker of the moment, careering off to out of the way places such as Chipping Norton in the Cotswolds. Our "Friday night is Crusader night" was a must, and of paramount importance. Attendance at those seemed to be the plumb line by which everything else was measured - a kind of "I got rhythm, have you got rhythm?" yardstick. In retrospect, very little happened singularly, apart from sleeping (even that was sometimes in each other's homes but only during school holidays), Saturday jobs, homework, exams and the odd (at times, very odd), boyfriend!.

It was a time of earnest (mainly!) evangelical fervour, with its overtones (and in low moments undertones!!). It taught me EVERYTHING - well, everything they wanted me to know for the time being, anyway. We were Top Dog in the singing of C.S.S.M. Choruses - (remember them, oh you of a certain age and persuasion?), the learning of scripture verses, particularly the memory verse of the week, and our geographical knowledge widening slightly as we became acquainted with the various missionaries we supported around the world. I still implored God not to send me to Africa (a childhood dread). The debate about the wearing of HETS - or hats if you're provincial, still circulated the Christian arena, forming a bone of contention as to whether females were suitably clad for the purposes of public worship. Try telling that to today's nearly naked brigade! The choruses were wonderfully inspiring, at least, I had always thought so, until my little delusionary bubble was burst at the most recent social gathering, some of the leaders admitting to never having liked them - what hidden treachery! As far as I was concerned, they (the choruses) had become the warp and weft of worship life. We sang them with gusto- well, actually with Roberta, Barbara, Ann, Christine, Sue, Amadine (sadly, no longer with us), Kath, Janice, Jenny, Janet, Linda and Jean. You'll see that I've deliberately broken up the alliteration, just to keep you on your toes! Other names spring to mind who swelled our evangelical ranks - Amanda with the huge brown eyes and from the Posh School, Cynthia (was she one of us at Crusaders or one of us at school? I've forgotten the link but not Cynthia!). There was Elizabeth and Jenny, whose mother hosted musical afternoons for us all (sadly now getting lost in the inner world of dementia- hope there's lots of music in there with her), Pat, who was at the most recent reunion looking quite glamorous, Annette, who became a missionary and her sister Maxine (who definitely did not!). Then there were the honorary members, Susan from school and whose parents ran an overseas students hostel (a kind of "male order" supply?) and Elaine, one of the Class missionaries we supported and who was once presumed dead during some trouble in Eritrea. She wasn't - dead that is, and came back to our city to prove it. I remember all the fervent prayers and tears at the assumed memorial service of thanksgiving for her life, perhaps prematurely organized but with the happiest of outcomes. Like the daffodils, there were a host of girls whose names (and faces!)

now escape me but whose presence added to the diversity yet unity of our tight knit squadron of God's faithful soldiers.

We were structured (possibly a bit straight jacketed on reading what I've just written) but we were young, eager to please and the product of the post war society which, after the assault on its very fabric, determined that we should be part of the glue that would help stick everything back together. After all, wasn't part of the content of our praises to God still concerned with us being the infantry in a war? Weren't we being urged on to win The Battle in which we were all engaged? Weren't we wielding swords and wearing breastplates and helmets, preferably of the metaphorical kind that we could use in our fight against The Foe? That same society was blissfully unaware of a bombshell of a different kind about to be dropped on it. A seismic cultural revolution was lurking, much like the pale, disaffected youths of my childhood, round the corner. The effects of this would be to empower youth in a way hitherto unimagined. Music, fashion, spending power and morality spearheaded radical change, engineered by an increasingly challenging youth movement, every bit as single minded as Germany's had been during the war, but differing in its intention and fuelled by Pop Music and its rising stars. Even Good Little Girls were going to be influenced by the new social currency. I expect our elders and betters were shivering in their shoes as to the effect the new radicalism would have on us all!

Despite the best efforts of parents and educators (I use that term generously), sex, like an unwelcome weed, tried to rear its mutinous head between the cracks of the evangelical pavement. It didn't seem to catch on, at least, not initially. Perhaps all that waging against war (on all fronts!) had stunned our hormones into total inactivity. Having to compete with the rousing command that "The Lord hath need of me, His soldier I will be" was not exactly the aphrodisiac that would light the fires of teenage passion. Maybe that was success in itself, for parents, teachers and leaders of youth, at any rate! I am strangely reminded at this point of the infamous Jackie, the Jessie James of our school. Her rating and reputation were on a par with the likes of Naughty Boy Mick Jagger, at least, to my mind. I was, at this stage, as legalistic and proprietorial as any biblical Pharisee to say the least. It would take a good few life experiences to knock the leopard- like spots off my being! She, Jackie, was hauled up on stage at an assembly and expelled - yes, expelled in front of our very eyes! A model of modernity, the comprehensive school of our town fathers' dreams had failed spectacularly in its brief to educate all on the parallel lines of democracy. Tram lines, phone lines, ley lines (spelt differently, this could have been the key to Jackie's most heinous crime!) had all reached meltdown in the eyes of the headmistress. It was something to do with the removal of her beret (there we go again, that "hat being a symbol of female chastity" thing). I hope it was nothing as trivial as pinching a Chewy from the sweet shop! I suspect it was more to do with the removal of rather more garments than a hat. The proverbial rug and plug were pulled triumphantly from under the hapless (and probably hatless) victim's feet. The bell didn't save her and nor can I remember it tolling. No, The Girl Did Wrong and out she shuffled. Actually, she didn't. She bounced off that stage, head held high in a last defiant gesture, cocking a snook at girls and teachers alike. I can almost hear the renegades of the repressed cheering, much like those at the guillotines in Paris, the only difference being that no one shouted "off with her head". We may have muttered, "The Head's off hers" - head, trolley, rocker - didn't matter, as long as the floor-show used up some of double maths time! I suspect she went on to have a glittering career (Jackie, that is), possibly on the wrong side of the tracks.

I wonder how many of you have the guts to admit to all those happy hours listening to Children's Favourites? (yes you did!). Saturday mornings invariably meant the bath time and hair wash ritual, me straining to hear my name called out on the radio downstairs - that's if my mum or dad (yeah, right!) had sent in a request to Uncle Mac. I always wanted "Sparky and the Magic Piano" or "There once was an ugly duckling" by Danny Kaye. You may remember that great song "the runaway train went down the track and she blew"? Well, that's precisely what Jackie did. She went down the track, ignored the signals, jumped over the buffers and without a backward glance but possibly with two fingers in the air, indicated, "blow you!" (or words to that effect). Whilst temporarily becoming a folk hero, the drastic action meted out to Jackie acted as an object lesson to all of us who wished to throw our berets into a hedge - or who, more seriously, wanted to Make Something Of Ourselves (that sounds suspiciously like Parent Speak). Berets had to be firmly clamped on our heads AT ALL TIMES, along with our aspirations. I was recently reminded by that closet rebel, Roberta that she folded hers, (the beret, not necessarily the aspirations!) pancake style and gripped it in place, ready to run the gauntlet of daily beret inspection by the sixth formers who positioned themselves on both front and back gates of the school. "Well I never, our Riberta!" (that was Gran Speak- Roberta's, that is). Concerning the daily Beret Run, the biblical imperative that it was easier to go through the eye of a needle comes to mind!

Talking of things biblical, it's sad to think that Jackie wasn't able to take refuge (within the school gates, at any rate) in Rowland's

Hut. She probably wasn't even thinking along those lines (there they go again!). She wanted to be out, not in and she certainly got her wish. Perhaps she sought and found sanctuary in a different direction. To be fair, she wasn't given the choice on life's nursery slopes that is school (even Big School) to find security, if not her identity. Her fate, like Stevie Wonder's song was signed, sealed and delivered. Yes, she was supposedly a Bad Girl of the time but where was the second chance? Maybe she'd had one. Perhaps she, like the proverbial cat had used up her nine lives. It's a good job that we're urged to forgive seventy times seven (too many numbers to juggle with here. Let's just settle for a lot, of forgiving that is!).

As far as the topic of Boy Crusaders went (that's an obscure segue!), it would seem they had been hidden somewhere behind a metaphorical brick wall, possibly in our famous city gates! I believe we never so much as crossed swords with any. I do recall that someone called Jerry led the local class but the name doesn't have a face, at least not in my memory! We soldiered on in our separate gender groups, singing, praying, learning memory verses and generally marching down life's highway together. The pinnacle of all this activity were the annual camps - oh yes, there were camps! They weren't the tented variety but the indoor house party types. These were held in the Easter and Summer holidays in the boarding schools of the well-bred of Britain. They were the "sleeping in a dorm and healthy pursuits" kind of holiday, with a Christian ethos. Bible study and mountain climbing went hand in hand, together with swimming, gardening, walking, sightseeing, shopping, local church going and the making of firm friendships with like-minded females. In retrospect, the camps were probably one big ticking menstrual clock, with the hands at the eleventh hour! The leaders of these camps were the evangelical equivalent of the Catholic Brides of Christ, but without the obligatory wedding ring. These particular handmaids of the Lord were free to fly the coup, flee the nest or tie the knot with any knight in shining armour that happened to ride into town but preferably with evangelical credentials. They could exchange selfless duty for, well, selfless duty!

As for us, as the song says, "Here come the Girls". Fresh faced and enthusiastic, we all took off on a togetherness trip that was to see us through our sometimes muddled, sometimes focussed teenage years. This was accompanied by faith, hope and chips - lots of them! That fooled your sense of Scripture, didn't it? Actually, the charity was there as well, considering our callow youthfulness and emerging female characters. Please remember that though we were we were the product of the faintly repressed, perhaps quite repressed - dammit, gym-slip repressed nineteen fifties, we were hurtling towards the sixties of Beatlemania! Wild horses, combined with John Cleese's famous herds of wildebeests sweeping over the plains of Torquay couldn't stop that particular dam of freedom from bursting all over our nicely pressed personalities - what a glorious mess! It was Pandora's Box, Jack in a Box and the Whole Box of Tricks in one fell swoop. Just what is a fell swoop? Is it the same as my asking, as a three year old, "what's a nanserdoo, Mummy? This was, of course, a misunderstood version of the popular song that demanded Daisy to "give me your answer, do"!

We were growing up at a time when the nation was leaving behind "the rule of the ration book", the legacy of a country at war. We were the Baby Boomers but unbeknown to our tender years, we were being prepared not only to Boom but to Rock – around the clock if Bill Hayley had his way! We were also going to twist and shout, do the mashed potato and perform various other rebellious gyratory expressions. These would enable us to thumb our noses at society and help stave off teenage boredom. We already had Elvis and Cliff, with the biggest sixties revolution quietly gathering speed but still out of sight, Man! We were witnessing the recreation of our city, slowly rising like the proverbial phoenix out of the smash-and-grab, tit-for-tat, broken-and-drab heartland, the legacy of the second world war. From the ashes rose our New Jerusalem, a concrete and glass wonderment, where its citizens could obtain the objects of the new currency of sixties life. The angular furniture and angular haircuts were offered from angular and, let's face it, downright ugly angular, plate glass buildings. We were being offered a new transparency, a reaction from all the covert practices needed for the war effort. However, like The Emperor's New Clothes, we accepted it all in the name of progress, which, after the previous devastation, was a paradise of modern affluence. Like the rosebay willow herb that had proliferated over the bomb-damaged sites, the citizens were undeterred in their quest for "improvement", and improve they did! The car factories flourished, as did the rise of The Foreign Holiday. It was the political era of "you've never had it so good" and I expect, for many, this was true. Added to this burgeoning regeneration was the presumed crowning glory of the city's historical legacy. The barefaced pink and plastic nudity of Lady Godiva travelled in and out of the clock tower as the clock struck each hour. She did this mounted on her equally plastic horse, shaking, rattling and rolling and thus providing a cheap and plastic thrill. Hopefully, this did not represent everyone's concept of things past. Not all hearts went "Boom, boody boom" a la Peter Sellers, or any other cheeky chappies!

As for the little maids, we were witnessing, with shock and awe (as the Americans now say) the re-building of the cathedral that had lost its roof but not its heart. There was renewed desire for it to be a testimony to God and a meeting place for His people. Each week we would make our pilgrimage past the site, observing its progress and marking our territory, before sharing our fish and chip tea in our city's famous eatery. This heralded our Friday nights together. What was Friday night? Of course, dear reader - it was Crusader Night! In retrospect, our cathedral pilgrimage was an essential part of our experience, squaring our spiritual circle and setting a seal upon our lives. The building was fast becoming the symbol of Reconciliation around the world. It must be said that it was also going to be a jolly good tourist attraction with its new hymns of ringing cash registers! As a young and shiny Girl Guide, I carried the patrol flag at an inaugural service and Roberta was chosen to read a bible passage at yet another such service. We acquitted ourselves well as the earnest representatives of our new spiritual home. These days, we would probably have been wearing a t-shirt to the effect!

For all this burgeoning permissiveness, we were still the original little maids from school, both actual and - cross my heart and hope to die, theatrical. The school was going to perform The Mikado, and our evangelically enthused swarm all took to their allotted roles with relish (and maybe too much sauce?) or something vaguely approximating it, given the million, trillion rehearsals and the equivalent congealed evening meals later, with tonsillitis for afters. With unnerving clarity, I can remember what a who-flung-dung of a near fiasco the Mikado was - on a personal level, at any rate! Chosen to play Yum Yum, a lead role as one of the three little maids, I was ousted out of the first night before the thing hit the stage, due to a much more Japanese-ly simpering and Orientally oriented replacement. She was also the unwitting pawn (or should that be prawn?) in the Director's strange game of revenge. I suppose it would be too psychological to protest that she, the Director didn't like me? Yes, thought so. Anyway, Miss Simpering Geisha was The Manager's Special, The Dish Of The Day. I, on the other hand, was well and truly The Take Away Choice, The Carry Out (as they say in Scotland), The Deep Fried Failure in boiling oil! Denuded and rejected, I was required, nay, commanded to "beef up the band" of the chorus by belting out top A's (could have been B's) - from the wings. Perhaps there should have been a plague of them - bees, that is and on her house! (as someone who doesn't easily come to mind said in some play or other). Okay, it was probably Shakespeare - it usually is. He has to carry the can for most things literary! It was not a terribly gracious "Oh, for the wings of a dove" situation, apart from the wish to fly far away. It was an ignominious position for one deposed from her prominent role! I have since come to view what happened as a royal reprieve, or should that be woyal weprieve, taking into account the fact that Yum Yum had to snog the English teacher - no, not what you might be thinking! Appearing as Ko Ko, he still couldn't conquer the speech impediment that rendered him as Woy Webberly, the Wolls Woyce of Wep. He clearly didn't know his R's from his elbows!

P.S. The Woy Webberly bit is totally correct!

The Mikado came and went. A levels came and went and no, don't ask! In fact, it all came and went - sixth form, our school houses with Greek sounding names (an Alpha but no Omega), coffee and sticky buns at break time, (a few buns in ovens as well!), music and God (in more or less equal measure). The whole fabric of our time as eleven to eighteen year olds was being torn down, rolled up and thrown away, as it were. At least, that's what it felt like - a strange and lonely time, an anti-climax, a dismantling of all that had seemed familiar'. Like Paddington Bear, we were being given new labels, telling us that from now on, we would be "On Our Own". Colleges and Universities beckoned, those far away places with the strange sounding names, heralding the Last Goodbye of the Golden Girls. We were "Wimmin", going forth or in the immortal words of Linda, (ever the Show Girl) coming fifth and winning a bag of peanuts, this being an irreverent but humorous reference to Moses, by the way! (God saying to him" Go Forth", etc.). Presumably we were going forth to multiply? However, this would not be advisable before we were wage earning, well some of us anyway! The poor old cast of The Mikado was smitten with a strange disease, the main symptom being the patter of tiny feet ... theatrical form of Mad Cow Disease or Foot and Mouth, maybe? (Answers on a postcard, please). Perhaps the rising of the artistic temperament had much to do with the affliction but whatever the reason, there were certainly fewer little maids at the start of the new school year! Just where did this world go? It seemed for many years to be like one of those villages submerged under water. We all knew it had once existed but had been consigned to the shadows of our minds. There had been the odd re-union that not all had managed to attend and of course, the funerals...

2007-2008 saw the Crusader Babes hit their 60th birthdays... surely not? Roberta's birthday gathering, unlike Humpty Dumpy, saw the Gels put back together again, some of them, anyway. In the blink of an eye, we became an unrehearsed but suitably earnest choir of fourteen year olds anxious to tell the urbane, post-modern gathering that "The Lord Hath Need Of Me (edited!).... And then one day His face I'll see, and oh, the joy when He says to me Well Done, my brave Crusader!" Our audience, taken by utter surprise at this somewhat naive offering clapped and beamed, shaken and stirred as thoroughly as any cocktail by this unexpected Call to Arms! As self-consciousness began to spread over us like an insidious and unwelcome hot flush (nothing changes), it begged the question as to whether we still meant those teenage expressions of faith? You bet we did! Well, some of us did and I expect it may have blown the dust off some people's faith. Can we carry on meaning it? Like Bob the Builder, Yes We Can! Such simplicity of expression suffused us with the determination to follow The Master of our spiritual formative years. With hindsight, (everyone's favourite friend), I've come to realise what happened in those few but vital minutes. Like an inflatable bouncy castle, up popped the Rowland's Hut that had been erected over us all those years ago. Until this moment, it had been packed away, each person having stored a bit of it in the dark recessed cupboard of her mind. Previously, other occasions had not lent themselves for such an invocation and response to take place. This time, we found ourselves once again seamlessly welded together, the process allowing each of us to be whom and what we have always been. As the saying goes, "you can't buy that for love or money" (as the Beatles knew only too well), not to mention the proverbial gold clock!

At the time of writing, the Girl Crusaders Union is about to be wound up. Now, if that's the case, shouldn't the clock (proverbial, gold, wrist or wall mounted) whose hands are pointing to the eleventh hour, be winding down? Not so! Even though "The Times They Are A Changing", (like the sentiments of Bob Dylan's plaintive song), it doesn't cancel out all that strong backbone of faith created by the stalwarts who presented, encouraged and stood for the Christianity they espoused. The leaders, tweed suited and mainly of single status, did not exactly establish themselves as the fashion icons of our faith world. What they did do was to pinpoint a recognisable movement, solid, dependable in its delivery of evangelicalism and a rock, however immovable and seemingly impervious to the perceived needs of a "me" generation of teenagers (wasn't it ever thus?). However, on the plus side, I do think we were still fairly pliable, willing to submit to our elders and mostly able to have huge respect for them, respect for older people still being at a premium. This is largely unlike the Today generation, to whom we are basically invisible unless sat upon in a cubicle at Primark! Being in such a retail establishment only adds fuel to the raging fire of intolerance. That we walk the face of the earth is a crime in itself, let alone that we may need to move around it to buy things! Where the fashion gap between the generations may have narrowed over the years, the sartorial shouldn't be used as the yardstick of spirituality. I don't think that's what "an outward and visible sign of an inward and spiritual grace" really means! It's more to do with what an eminent "man of the cloth" famously described as, "the main thing is keeping the main thing and that's the main thing. He was, of course, referring to the passage where we are urged to love the Lord Your God with all your heart, soul, mind and strength and your neighbour? Well, as yourself, of course..!

I heard recently on Premier Christian Radio that Crusaders has been re-branded as Urban Saints. Now, if this is the same Crusaders as known and loved by either The Girls, the Boys or even the maverick "mixed" bunch, all power to its new "moniker"! What's a bit of re-branding between friends, especially if it "Calls to Arms" a whole new marching generation? Being pragmatic, I would imagine that it's highly likely that this evolutionary step belongs to what was the more progressive mixed gender groups. I heard from a particular horse's mouth about the actual disbanding of the wing under which we sheltered. I should imagine it goes without saying that gatherings will be mixed in gender, worship conducted to the rock beat that governs most contemporary worship songs and nothing anachronistic used in the choice of teaching material. You can almost hear a deep sigh of envy but not necessarily mine! Some of the oldies are still definitely the goldies, despite seemingly outmoded language, rhythm and idiom. After all, it's people who have shifted culturally and linguistically, not God! His time paradigm isn't ours - a thousand years being as a day, etcetera. He's just pleased to receive our praise, as long as it's in spirit and truth. Worship is the ultimate area in which" one man's ceiling is very definitely another man's floor" (thank you, Paul Simon, as always, for being a succinct word-smith). I couldn't have put it better myself.

Whatever happens to the re-branded, revamped and probably re-logo'd organization, it will always remain in my heart and soul, my Forever England. Just as we were encouraged to be what is now termed "pro active" in our evangelising style (not totally "me", I hasten to add), so the succeeding generations also will be. I hope "Urban Saint-ing" pays dividends to all those committed leaders. As for myself, I can still (if I want to) wear my badge with pride, a bit battered and bent (like the owner!) but still symbolizing that ultimate outward sign of belonging. Maybe I'll be wearing it when God says to me, "Well done, my brave Crusader!"

Since I began this chapter, Pauline, our very own Golden Girl, had finished her earthly journey. Pauline Gwendoline Anne, our school music teacher and Girl Crusader leader was the friend and confidante of many. She was my spiritual mother and one of the significant giants of faith in my life. She pointed the Way and dispensed love and chocolate peppermint creams in equal measure. We recently gathered to say farewell to her, and once again, Rowland's Hut covered and moulded us into that earnest and spirited band of pilgrims. Au Revoir Pauline and like you, Jesus will meet us standing on that Shore!

Chapter 4: Long Live Joie de Vivre

"And you'll see roses in the snow, then Joie de Vivre will make them grow."
- The Sherman Brothers

I celebrated my 21st birthday at my College of Education, or in old money, Teacher Training College. It was the 1960's, and it was still the Age of Majority, the "Key of the Door" thing. It certainly was - an education, that is, and I'm still trying to work out who was educating whom, if "Leggy Reggy" (student) and the English tutor were an example! Put it this way - it gave a whole new perspective to the meaning of a personal tutor, and also in putting the "man" in manoeuvres. Additionally, there was the predictable "tutor luvs tutor" activity, and it became the norm to see yet another male English tutor knocking furtively on the door of a certain female modern dance tutor, before evaporating through it. Just what was with those English tutors? I guess they had a way with words.....

As was the tradition of the time, the college students were all female - more of the same for those of us who had spent our secondary education days in single gender cloisters. The inevitable upshot was the mass exoduses to the testosterone charged male bastion of the agricultural college a coach ride away, with the return match (as it were) being played on our home turf. I will never forget the culture shock - and every other shock, of an evening gyrating to Jumping Jack Flash, by The Stones, at a nearby university. That truly was Space Cadet City! In fact, the whole of our college days seemed a surreal mix of lectures, Tamla Motown music, lectures, school practice times, lectures, trips to buy Charlie boots and kinky boots, lectures, the illicit smuggling of male persons in and out of the building we were forced to call home - oh, and more lectures!

Anyway, back to my birthday. My friends had plastered the walls with computerised sheets of paper containing the words "knickers knockers" all over them. Why? Je ne sais quois, as our friends across the channel say. Well, it was the psychedelic Sixties and anything seemed to go! It's brought to mind a Christian speaker's young son who was with his family on our teaching weekend in Wales. He spent his time in the corridors of the country pile we were staying in, shouting "Knickers Norris, Knickers Norris". I suspect that taunting him with his surname (the Norris bit!) was a playground thing, and he was taking the opportunity to try his shock tactics out on us - or maybe to humiliate his dad. Whatever the reason, it has the same uncanny ring about it as my birthday greeting! My friends bought me a perfume gift set, and its name was - yes, you've guessed it, "Joie de Vivre", a pale blue liquid in clear glass bottles. Isn't it strange that, even after all this time, I can still recall the fragrance? It's amazing how we can do that!

The definition of Joie de Vivre is "the cheerful enjoyment of life, the exultation of spirit". For me, it was like that Post War sing-along song from across The Pond, asking us to "Put another nickel in, In the Nickelodeon, All I want is lovin' you and music, music, music". At this point, I need to wind the tape back to a time long before the days of college, even further back before the days of secondary school, and way, way back down that dusty corridor of time, to my early years on the planet. I don't think there was actually a beginning to my love affair with music. It was always in me, and me in it, with the metronome seemingly always ticking. It was my Day Star, my Lode Star, and possibly even my "Telstar" - go on, admit that you remember that one, oh you and I of the Sputnik revolution! As far back as I can remember, music made sense, held me together, connected all things and claimed my soul.

My pre-school days were punctuated by "Housewives Choice" and "Listen While You Work" on the radio. They were daily programmes of cheerful, inspiring music that began in the War days of 1940, and running until the 1960's. The music was also played to the workers in the factories, encouraging them to keep up production, and to boost the morale of the nation, the musicians having such exotic names such as "Troise and his Banjoliers" and "Bernard Monshin and his Rio Tango Band". Each day, "Housewives Choice" would end with the compère, George Elrick, singing to the signature tune with his own jingle: "Doodle dum de doodle dum", and ending with "And I'll be with you all again tomorrow morning". Even though I've had to check the names and details, I remember it all vividly. It was all a regular, melodic rhythm of life - and it was deliciously reassuring. Then there was my friend's mother, working away at home and bellowing out "The Holy City", known as "Jerusalem" (not THAT Jerusalem of the flag waving, Last Night of the Proms variety!) over her washing up. It was a noble stirring, a call to arms! Sunday School was the source of my musical" sunbeam" moments, singing those hymns where Jesus wanted me to be one - a sunbeam, that is! Uncle Mac guaranteed to spread personal joy all over my Saturday morning. His "Children's Favourites" on the radio went hand in hand with my bath and hair wash sessions, soap suds and musical happiness covering me in equal measure. It was my introduction to a lifetime's inner supply of spiritual oil

- my cheerful enjoyment, the exultation of my spirit, my very own Joie de Vivre that was music.

My Infant school days introduced me to those lovely little hymns of uncomplicated, childlike trust in God, where, for once in my life, the words and melodies needed each other and I needed both. My early junior school days were interrupted by the tonsil problems that were to dog me for several years. However, in having to spend time at home, I soon discovered another musical joy. In watching the static television test card, (I'm afraid we had to make do with that as our morning programme!), I was stopped in my already sedentary tracks by the accompanying music. It was none other than Mozart's "Eine Kleine Nachtmusik". It was astounding - the sound, the mathematical structure (I didn't recognise it as such at that point, maths not even having a place on my horizon!) the ordered discipline and the perfectly crafted melodic lines.

It was a new sound-scape, an escape route into another era that I knew nothing about with my mind, but which I recognised with my spirit. It wasn't anything I could, or even needed, to share. It was my new little world, a high gate to a secret garden that I could return to each day. It could be reached through the little brown Bakelite box with the minuscule screen, that Holy Grail of modernity that was positioned, like an altar, in a corner of the room of our Fifties house. It also came with my father's Eleventh Commandment attached to it, "Thou canst look but Thou must not touch", It came before the days of remote controls which offer the freedom to "zap" any channel you want. I was forbidden to touch either of the control knobs that consisted of "on and off" and "something else", possibly volume or that mysterious, unknown (to my mind) quantity, "contrast", consequently heightening my lifelong technophobic tendencies!

For a technically challenged person, I was strangely attracted to, and totally understood the music tabulators (hope you're suitably impressed!) that hung on the walls of my junior school music room, displaying the tonic sol-fa, (the phonic sounds of the scale). It is a perpetual mystery as to why these seemed so natural when other indecipherable symbols such as arithmetic jumped up and bit me! Maybe it was to do with the redoubtable Mrs Campling, whose methods of music teaching were thorough, a "no-nonsense in an upper class ladylike way" manner, yet strangely inspiring. She was not a sufferer of fools, gladly, lightly or anything else that ended in "ly"! The memory of "fools rushing in where angels" etc, is well and truly etched, like an inky black tattoo, on the bit of my brain marked Primary School. A hapless, and probably helpless boy blew his nose and what was even worse, proceeded to rummage around in the grubby rag that predated tissues. He was right under the aforesaid teacher's own nose. Then came the shot across the bows, the "if the cap fits, wear it" moment. She looked over the edges of her spectacles (I'm surprised it wasn't a lorgnette), drew herself up to full height, and enunciated in the best Queen's English, "one must not scan the contents of one's handkerchief".....I can assure you, hand on heart, that this was completely true.

A much more humane teacher, with the pretty name of Mrs Appleby, taught the recorder to beginners. I quickly qualified for the preliminary group but longed - with the kind of "gluing myself to the windows of the hall" longing, to be a part of "The Proper Ensemble", my face squashed up against the glass, my ears straining to hear the impact of the sounds, my eyes taking in the body movements of the group. This was no mere "tootling along" scenario, no siree! The ensemble comprised descant, treble, tenor and bass recorders, their prowess winning them prizes in music festivals. The pieces were sophisticated classical renditions, the extremely mysteriously named "In A Deep Vaulted Cell" firing my imagination. I later discovered that it's from "Dido And Aeneas", the operatic story of The Queen of Carthage and the Prince of Troy, by the seventeenth century Baroque composer, Henry Purcell. One of its key arias is "When I am laid in earth". There's not a lot to commend that, is there?

After much window gazing, I eventually earned a place in that coveted elite, acquiring all the skills of disciplined ensemble playing, and finding out first hand the thrill of competing in the festivals and winning First place! The commitment had to be total, the teacher being the one mentioned in another chapter as the inspiring teacher of English. I had arrived in creative Heaven! The only down side to the situation was not being allowed to be in both ensemble and choir, my other great aspiration in life. It must have been based on the thinking that you couldn't achieve both successfully. It was an early taste of having to choose, but I do think it was somewhat arbitrary in nature, as lots of people like to express themselves through both mediums. Even so, recorder playing at an advanced level afforded me so much, sharpening my skills and knowledge, and providing a group dynamic and identity that gave definition to my junior school life. It certainly allowed my spirit to be exulted, and I clearly had an enjoyment of life. Joie de Vivre was alive and well!

With secondary school came the demotion of recorder playing and the fulfilling of my choral aspirations. It was at this juncture that my piano playing desires were factored in. The whole piano lessons venture felt like a runaway horse, where I was forever galloping over, under, and round the sticks! Because I had begun to learn at a relatively late stage, I always felt like there was too much catching up to do and consequently approached everything at breakneck speed. Had I practised consistently, I might have achieved more, instead of my "less is more" philosophy, combined with my "it's more or less okay" attitude! As our good friend says, Hey Ho! I really feel it was the uniquely delicious sticky buns, sold through the open sixth form windows, that were my carrot and stick on piano lesson mornings. I've never encountered any like them (buns, that is) and I'm left wondering as to whether it was actually Manna from Heaven........

The time came to put away childish things, so, off with the old and on with the new. In actual fact, College was possibly a case of The King's New Clothes (courtesy of Danny Kaye). What were essentially still little girls (at heart), they paraded as fully fledged grown ups, teetering around on high heels and sporting the mini dresses, huge false eyelashes and hairpieces that dominated our sixties' fashion skyline At the same time, there was much crying in college phone boxes over lots of male spilt milk, and the longing to just go home, and be once more washed, fed and looked after in their parental Rowland's Huts. Oh, the contradictions of making your own bed and having to lie on it! On better days, those same young things were full of chutzpah, ready to tough it out with boyfriends, kids in their school practise class, financial assets that disappeared at an alarming rate, or simply survival on an all female campus. On those days, the Joie was exceedingly Vivre!

Soul Music, under the label of Tamla Motown, was the ingredient in the mix of all college life, binding it together into a sometimes sweet and sticky, sometimes dry and crumbly cake. There was the coffee - like stimulant of The Isley Brothers singing "Behind The Painted Smile", accompanying our every early morning coach journey for six weeks. It nursed us on our way to our various schools, where we were "practising" our embryonic skills. On our return, the strains of "Reach Out, I'll Be There" by The Four Tops floated down our corridor, anaesthetising the stresses of the day and re establishing a sense of college-style equilibrium. My predilection for all things classical had to largely remain under wraps in my hall of residence, or at least played at minus one on my record player, not having the benefit of iPods and mp3's in those technically dim and distant days! My allegiance was expressed within the walls of the block where I studied music, one of my two specialist subjects, the other being the Art of Movement (Dance), the two going hand in hand. At least, they should have done. It's sufficient to say that the tutor and I didn't exactly share a relationship bathed in sweetness and light! Despite that hiccup, music, in all the colours and all the sizes, remained my passion, my reason, my total Joie de Vivre. It anchored me, restored me, inspired me, and rose up through my being like an underground stream bubbling up into a cascading, shimmering waterfall. It was my medicine, my gift from God. Furthermore, the music tutor liked me - and that always helps!

The music students regarded its department as the beating heart of their world, and even the whole college. It was an oasis amongst the academic scrum, an ecosystem sustaining and nourishing all those fuelled by the crotchets and quavers that created such beauty and inner meaning. Its walls seemed to have absorbed sounds of both past and present, emitting them through its pores, and urging us on to greater creativity. It witnessed music that not only moved us but astounded us in equal measure. There was the small local boy from a Caribbean family, brought in to display his astonishing, if puzzling gift. It was in the same vein as the small child who could draw the Houses of Parliament after a cursory showing of a picture. This little boy, although academically challenged, could reproduce any work for piano after just one hearing. It floored everyone, especially those of us who were academically endowed but pianistically challenged! We certainly needed tea and sympathy that day!

The release of Sergeant Pepper's Lonely Hearts Club Band caused a Joie of the highest Vivre! We were unexpectedly introduced to it at our music department's Christmas bash - by the Head of the department, no less. How about that for eclectic and crossover? I can still see us dancing - round our handbags, round the chairs, and round just about everyone and everything else in the room. The opening chords that announced "With A Little Help from Our Friends", gave us no choice but to be propelled up onto the dance floor, in celebration of our mop haired heroes. As we used to say, It was FAB!

The function of the department went far beyond that of academic rigour and artistic achievement. I clearly remember the feeling of leaving the fragmented world of college behind as I went through the department door. It was similar to the children in "The Lion, The Witch And The Wardrobe" by C.S. Lewis, Like them, we found our Narnia - a better life behind the door. The Head of Department became surrogate mother to the distressed and the temperamental, calming and soothing the wounded, and the wound up females of the species. Her tutorial room was a sanctuary, a confessional, a Rowland's Hut of warmth and common sense, where cups of tea prevailed over high drama and the many perceived tragedies, worthy of any grand opera! All would be forgiven and forgotten as they immersed their souls in the joint choral performances, singers and audience alike being captivated and transported by such works as Brahms' Zigeuner Lieder (Gypsy Songs). Having listened to it again, I can hardly believe I sang it, such is the vocal discipline needed and which, sadly, has largely departed. Music and drama faculties occasionally collaborated, possibly colluded but definitely collided! One highly memorable meshing of talent resulted in "The Beggar's Opera", by John Gay, a satirical comment on politics, poverty and injustice. It proved to be a thrilling display of both vocal and acting talent, and although on one level it pains me to say it, the vocal quality of the drama department at least equalled those of us who thought we'd cornered the market!

A friend recently told me that she had spent most of her life feeling like she was two people. Having moved at the age of twelve from what must have felt like a northern outpost, she'd been shamed into perfecting an alternative accent in order to be accepted in a new, and apparently derisory branch of society. Consequently, she has become "bilingual", moving from one accent to the other, triggered by the person she happened to be with at the time. She now wishes that she had been brave enough to stick to her guns, and her roots, instead of having hidden the background which had formed her and which still restores her Joie de Vivre purpose. The balancing of two worlds is a more common feature of our existence than we first think. I realise that I did precisely the same thing with my life at college, adapting accordingly to either the friends outside, or those within the Christian faith.

In retrospect, the two worlds differed widely. Those with faith offered a different kindness and tolerance that emanated from a different place - gentler, ethically more reliable, and it has to be said, purer! During my times of fear and uncertainty and an absence of both Joie and Vivre, they were always there to welcome me into Rowland's Hut for restoration, and believe you me, I definitely needed that place to retreat to. My other friends had the world's tendency to sell you down the river, should you not be their flavour of the week. I wish those young Women of The Faith could now be told that they did actually "shine like stars" in that jumbled heap of female humanity. I only hope they've all managed to maintain their beliefs, as life and choices in the real world began to make its demands. God bless the Paulines, the Dianes, the Christines, and the Annes from those heady days of the sixties, who "walked the walk and talked the talk". Now that we are all in our own sixties, I hope that they have all continued as Hut people, offering love and kindness to those who may have lost their way, their happiness and their appetite for living in this often tearful and fearful spinning globe. As the song says, the "roses in the snow" can blossom, and the Joie de Vivre, that love of life, can be restored. Despite the most difficult circumstances, a cheerful enjoyment of life can be attained, where love can melt the ice, and kindness is able to thaw the frozen heart.

The end of college didn't mean the end of musical joy, or any other joy. I had met my future husband, who was a guitarist, and a Christian, so the signs were good! He belonged to the local folk club, where he was one of the regular singers and it wasn't long before we'd joined musical forces. I quickly absorbed some of the folk music repertoire, and finding it natural to sing harmonies, a new duo was born. My husband crafted his own songs, some of them finding their way into other artists' repertoires, always a highly gratifying accolade. One of the spin-offs from this was the request from my husband's old school friend and fellow folk artist, to write and perform the music for the film he was submitting for his art college final exam. The subject was the knocking down of Canny Street in Sheffield, and the subsequent dismantling of a long established community. The film, interspersed with interviews of the locals, showed them voicing their anger at the tearing down of their homes - their "Rowland's Huts", and their fears for the future, not least their rehousing. The music we wrote was a blend of ethereal beauty and the reflection of pragmatic inevitability, woven around the social commentary. I don't think we ever saw the finished article, but I hope it did the trick and gained our friend his academic and artistic stripes. The last we heard about him was that he was involved in making films of a much more dubious nature - hope he didn't think he was still being "canny".....

Folk music is a compelling and powerful oral tradition, pre-dating all that was later notated, its messages of social importance and stories of love and heartbreak being conveyed from one generation to another. The tradition lives on, the musical documenting of contemporary world events and social injustices still being committed to song. The folk revival of the mid to late 20th century was in its ascendancy, and we had the privilege of experiencing many fine artists and practitioners. It has to be said that folk musicians are a highly skilled bunch of artisans, portraying and practising their craft with deceptive ease. They are the masters of the stand up, the easy banter, and the adaptability needed to play the part of the travelling troubadour. We became part of the regular local musicians, those stalwarts who are the backbone and lifeblood of the local clubs, the ready supply of emerging talent who faithfully show up for "Singers' Nights". To my never ending amazement, some of those now pop up on YouTube, their considerable abilities still able to "tell a tale" and to keep the wheels turning. As they say, keep on truckin', my friends! Our particular club went down in history as the outfit who turned down Paul Simon, no less! In its defence, it was still in the early days of his career, with his reputation not having quite gone before him. As they say, the rest was history, the egg still rolling down the club's collective face long after Simon's meteoric rise to fame! On the up side, if Art Garfunkel had appeared, I doubt his hair, or even his name for that matter, would have made it through the narrow door!

The folk club, with its music and members gave me the sense of the Joie de Vivre I'd found all those years ago. Again, it was another personal secret garden of musical delights, along with all the characters, in all the colours and definitely in all the sizes. The latter had as much to do with the amount of beer consumed which, together with the cigarettes, formed the staple diet of "dyed in the wool" folkies - their "five a day"! The music took us beyond the walls of the club, to festivals, Morris Meets (yes, those good ol' boys of the jingling bells, floral hats, and beer tankards dangling from their persons!), to playing on a lorry at the town's annual carnival and like Muzac or Karaoke, having to sing the same song over, and over, and really over again! By the time we'd sung "Then to the maypole, haste away" fifty million, trillion times, I wanted to take that maypole and toss it, like the proverbial caber, over the side of the lorry. Happy days!

Every organisation has its living legends, our folk club being no exception. Hector from the Highlands worked for the Milk Marketing Board, his day job concealing his true vocation. He had the voice of a Scottish angel and the ability to whisk us away to the lochs and mountains of his homeland. "Heel ya ho, boys, let her go, boys, heave her head round to the weather, - "was his "Mingalay Boat Song" clarion call to his fellow exiles, and also to us, the Sassenachs - the Saxon villains of the piece. The effect of "The Wild Mountain Thyme" was akin to the singing of "Jerusalem" or "You'll Never Walk Alone", evoking a Jingoism that you wouldn't have thought existed in such a "Whisky In The Jar" environment. Talk about seeing grown men cry......I still think the nostalgia was mainly beer glass shaped! Imagine our recent surprise when Hector, one of those home purveyors of musical goodies, popped up on our iPad, still with the same vocal clarity and appeal, and still bringing joy.

Then there was Wilse, not so much a living legend as a One Man Saviour of the brewing industry! As the evenings rose, Wilse fell - over chairs, over people, and even over himself. It's a wonder he didn't fall down the stairs (the club was held in an upper room of a pub - and where have you heard that before, apart from the pub bit?) on his beer runs to the bar below. Had he done so, he probably wouldn't have broken anything other than his beer glass, owing to his increasingly anaesthetised state. In any case, he was one of the more passive types when "under the influence", rendering him harmless, if not armless! His musical contribution was of the "yo ho ho and a bottle of rum", unaccompanied sea shanty variety, performed with plenty of aplomb, pzazz and plonk. We last saw him when we were revisiting the town we'd moved away from. He was getting on a bus, almost incognito with his big, bushy beard, but nevertheless still Wilse underneath. He seemed "clothed and in his right mind", to quote a famous biblical incident and was older, wiser, and seemingly, hairier! I hope his life is still inhabited by the musical "muse", and maybe less liquid libation?

The amount of Daves involved at the club were like the spots of a measles epidemic - say the name and they all came out. Perhaps the biggest "spot" has been Dave Warwick (nee Edwards - in the Equity sense!) who has had considerable success as an actor. We probably all shouted at our television screens when he popped up in a play, large as life and twice as "Dave", each of us claiming birthright, and rushing outside to erect a blue plaque, insisting that "Dave woz 'ere". With regard to ourselves, he certainly was 'ere, teaming up with him to sing "To Try For The Sun", made famous by Donovan but better known as "We Stood In The Windy City". In my estimation, it was the plaintive cry of a heart, daring to reach for the stars but only finding earth. As my Grandpa used to say, "You reach for the sky but all you get is the earth - Fuller's earth", another plaintive cry of the heart from another person with shattered dreams and a story to tell. It just goes to show that each one of us is a folk artist in our own right, with a life-catalogue of highs and lows, ups and downs, rises and falls.

Our reconnection with church going meant a heart searching decision to forgo our Sunday evening folk club habit. It was a bitter-sweet decision to exchange all that camaraderie and joyful musical involvement for our spiritual quest, but one we felt compelled to make at that point in our lives. In retrospect, that decision was a link in our chain, with one leading to another. The "roses in the snow" began to grow through a friendship cemented at the church. We were introduced to a new fellowship outside its walls, a very happy band of Christian pilgrims who helped us live through a time we came to regard as our "Golden

Days", and which like all our ventures, featured that sparkling, refreshing, effervescence that was music. It was a celebration and continuation of my Joie de Vivre!

Some years later, I was once more reconciled to my classical music roots, coaxing them back into life through my children's musical learning curve. As they progressed with their instruments, their repertoire increased and consequently so did the recovery of my classical appetite, leaving me wondering why I had allowed it to disappear, but very happy that it had returned! I recovered my pianistic skills (don't get too excited!), taught recorder to hoards of young hopefuls, and even ventured into the lion's den that is secondary school music teaching, experiencing the "thrill and fear" tightrope of creating, collaborating, and conducting The Christmas Concert. I survived, they survived and actually, I was very proud of them! I'm so glad that music has been the golden thread running through my life. I'm grateful for its benefits - its medicinal and healing properties, its logic, its ability to create emotional happiness, and to join people together. It's my gift! It's my Joie de Vivre!

Chapter 5: With A Little Help From My Friend

"Put your life on the line for your friends.........you are my friends when you do the things I command you ....I've named you friends because I've let you in on everything I've heard from the Father."
- John 15 v15 (The Message version of The Bible)

It had been dubbed "The Squash". It came into our lives at a time when our church of choice didn't seem to be delivering. With the high handedness of youth, we flounced out of a conversation with the church secretary (poor man - we now burn with shame!) and on to pastures new. Not wishing to influence us, our friends had been diplomatically waiting for us to ask them about a meeting they went to. The gathering was regarded as suspect by the aforesaid church, but this was the catalyst that propelled us towards, rather than away from, the dangling carrot. Even the rather tenuous connection with that Prince of Engineers, Isambard Kingdom Brunel, his descendants being members of the church, wasn't enough to hold us. In retrospect, it seems clear that the pathway we took was a choice that led us into the light, space and purposes God had for us.

A Methodist mission in the rural area surrounding Ken and Ruth's farm resulted in them gathering up the youth and creating a weekly meeting. It was held in the house on their beautiful farm and became a place of utter generosity and warmth. Christian speakers would visit to teach and example the faith, along with lively worship and the cementing of friendships which are alive and well today. Our host and hostess were lavish with their lives, ferrying people to and fro and offering those with vehicles to fill up from the petrol pump in the farmyard for free! Many social events took place outside this meeting, the result being Church without walls. We were gladly received into the happy band of pilgrims of mainly teenagers, even though we were twenty somethings and married. We certainly were packed cheek by jowl into the room, rather in the manner of sardines in a tin. In being Squash, we were most definitely squashed! It was at this juncture that we got to know Paul, he of "it's a load of old conkers" fame, his dad (who seemed to inhabit another realm) and his nephew Steven. Paul used to get very frustrated with teaching that didn't sound plausible to his ears, hence the occasional outbursts! Paul and Steve were guitarists and led the worship as well as performing Paul's song compositions. The latter was unmarried at that point but had a girlfriend, Christine who attended the Squash. It wasn't long before my husband, also a guitarist, joined forces with Paul and Steve to form The Good News Band, the one mentioned in another chapter. Kind Ken became their "roady", transporting band equipment (bought by Ken) in his nine seater Peugeot to gigs in faraway places with the strange sounding names! Ruth was an amazing force, combining motherhood with her many activities. Her four children were all in evidence on Squash nights, Andrew, Carolyn and Anne being part of the group. Young Mark was either running wild in the fields with his friend Keith, or trying to shrink the latest pair of jeans by wearing them in the bath, Ruth being heard muttering that she couldn't do anything with him! Her care was personal, making sure people were fed and watered, giving gifts to our new babies and numerous little kindnesses, all done in a no-nonsense way but with a generous heart. I still remember the beautiful blue romper suit she gave us on our son's arrival.

The meetings were invariably led by Rowland, a colourful character with a high pitched voice and a girlfriend called Maggie. Rowland's living arrangements were unorthodox, to say the least. He had moved out of the family house and had taken up residence in a huge hut in the garden. Once a chicken shed, it now housed Rowland, his bed, an assortment of antiques and a strange collection of items without obvious purpose! Undaunted, Rowland extended the midweek gathering on the farm to Sunday evenings after church. On arrival, he would yell at us all to make our own drinks, sending us across to the glass lean-to attached to the side of his parents house. Back in the hut, We would huddle round the ancient heating stove and sing, pray, share and bind ourselves together in togetherness and acceptance. It was these memories that sparked the quest to locate those times in my life that offered the same sense of belonging and acceptance I experienced in Rowland's hut.

How I took that time for granted - that time of my life and the life of my time! I remember the clever, pretty , friendly girls and the handsome, vital, fearless young men, all seeking a relationship with God and each other. There were the ups and downs of the boyfriend-girlfriend episodes, the birthday celebrations, the away days to the Albert Hall to the "Start the new year with Jesus" concerts and others nearer home, but having equal importance in our lives. It was an age of "being down there with the kids", worshipping at the feet of such luminaries as Larry Norman, Graham Kendrick, Trinity Folk and Canaan - whose home church in the north later became ours! There was the memorable occasion of the Millstone Grit gig where we had to squat and probably "squash" on the floor! At eight months pregnant, I was not a pretty sight, nor was it an entirely comfortable call!

Socially, the Squash operated in different ways. There were the times when it moved around like a swarm of bees, and then there were the smaller friendship groups, borne out of shared interests and age factors. John and Andrea, Keith and myself plus seventeen year old Cynthia, larger than life (and twice as difficult to handle) often found ourselves in, let's say, unorthodox situations. John was keen on sampling places of worship, one of these being a certain Pentecostal church. Fresh faced and unsuspecting, we turned up at the door to be greeted with the request, nay command, to give either our testimonies or to sing, this preceded by the possible locking and bolting of doors.....

This was still the era of hats being next to godliness. I don't know if there was a dressing up box at the door, but hats were duly provided and clapped on female heads, topping seventies smock tops and impossible platform shoes. I cannot bring myself to picture the collective sight, but suffice it to say, we would have blended in perfectly with the proceedings about to unfold. I'm going to fast forward to the incident of the collection. Let's call her The Girl With Green Hair, the lady of certain years, who doubled as musical entertainer and tax collector. She went off the pianistic Richter scale before changing literal and metaphorical hats, whereupon she extorted money by importunate means. Not happy with the contents of the swag bag, she once more circuited until she felt satisfied with the amount of jingle, with or without bells. As they say, follow that! We had to! Corralled and suitably clad, we stood like skittles, warbling our very apt "If ever there was just one day" rendition and waiting for the balls to knock us over. We managed to beat the retreat, shedding hats along with the remains of our dignity as we fled into the night.

My guess is that we took ourselves off to Freddie's, that Rowland's Hut of gastronomy. It wasn't the most usual setting (nothing of this era ever was), a Tudor style black and white building, housing a Chinese restaurant and run by a six foot oriental gentleman! It was, however the best Chinese food I have ever come across, the fifty nine with egg fried rice never failing to deliver, while the sweet and sour was the legendary stuff of dreams. Alas, like Yorick, Poor Freddie is no more, having coming to a not very sweet but exceedingly sour end on the mean streets of a nearby town. Reputably stabbed to death, we can but hope that the knife wasn't from his own kitchen. Thank you, Freddie for that small but perfectly formed Kubla Khan, your gastronomic pleasure dome, where we gathered with friends to celebrate our togetherness and love of food.

The invitation to go to Ivy Cottage to hear Dennis Clarke and Campbell McAlpine immediately invoked an image of a builders' convention in some rural idyll. In reality, Ivy Cottage was a city Baptist church, now re-branded as Ivy. I'm unclear as to the reason for the event, but I do remember that the teaching exhorted us not just to be human. We were to be Superhuman! I don't recall seeing underpants over trousers, and I'm still not sure whether being "more than conquerors" is one and the same thing, but it did leave me feeling more than exhausted! My guess is that we beat another retreat, and headed in the direction of Freddie's wonderful sanctuary. It was akin to today's Priory but without the hard work of rehab!

Our five-some, augmented by assorted musicians and other conscripts were sometimes seconded to the services of a fearless hard man. A teacher at what was known as the naughty boys school, this character ran a Christian Saturday night venture for bikers. We musicians would be made to stand on a table to perform, closely followed by the now familiar locking of doors. Man, beast, motor biker and us would be held captive as the hard man proceeded to strut his preaching stuff! His raison d'etre was, the more he was disliked, the more successful his evangelisation .... When the doors were finally unlocked, we decanted into the street, the night air fragrant after our compulsory imprisonment. We no doubt fell gratefully into the sweet without sour arms of Freddie, not caring whether he and his staff were dreamers or not! These evenings had all the innate charm of a Hieronymous Bosch painting and served to reinforce my aversion to that overt type of evangelism. This pick and mix selection was representative of the situations we seemed to fall into, led by John, our fearless if somewhat anachronistic friend. He was a man clearly ahead of his, and definitely our, theological time. He had read about, and perceived God in ways as yet unrevealed to the rest of us. We weren't fazed, accepting his relationship with God and the ways he expressed it as "that's just John"! The locking of doors seemed to figure prominently in our evangelistic efforts, not surprising when it came to our being invited to sing to prisoners. You begin to wonder how anyone manages to break out of prison in view of the amount of doors being locked behind you. It just had to have been God who sprang St. Paul out of his!

We had a temporary break from Squash life for a few months. We tried our hand at living in my original home city, leaving our unsold house and moving in with my parents. I was seven months pregnant with our second child, so it wasn't without its challenges. There was the transfer of crucial medical care, the confines of sharing a house and the overriding feeling of having lost our home to deal with. We'd also left the Rowland's Hut of friends and spiritual support. Without the imminent arrival of a new baby, life would have been decidedly monochromatic. My stress levels mounted when the unborn baby took it upon itself to perform gymnastics, resulting in it being in the wrong position. Medical doom and gloom was scattered around like Shake-n-Vac, retracted only after a Prod-n-Poke session by a group of earnest but only ever so slightly trained students. A previous prod from a world weary doc resulted in a wink and thumbs up over the slender shoulders of the search and rescue team. When our son made his appearance, the evidence of his Houdini inspired activity became clear. He had played loop the loop once too often, the cord being firmly wound round his neck and causing a tense few moments as he was carefully disentangled.

We reversed our move and returned to our own home, still unsold and waiting to receive us back. I was so grateful, so relieved, so happy to introduce our baby son to his home and to re acclimatise our twenty month old to the house he had gone home to as a newborn. I still remember the novelty of making a chocolate trifle and popping it in MY fridge, of leaving a pan of mince on the stove to burn itself (and us) into near oblivion.....

I soon regained my housewifely position and took to my autonomy like the proverbial duck. Our relationship with all things Squash and Hut was resumed and I revelled in normal domesticity, the everyday story of a seventies housewife and mum. In comparing it with today, it seems pedestrian, limited, undemanding. I had always wanted to wheel babies in springy prams, choose those delicious miniature outfits and to generally be Mum in all its colours and sizes. To me, it was a secure, defined and purposeful rhythm of baby and child rearing, of house tending and friend making. Some of these friends were the young girls from the Squash, popping up as if from nowhere. In reality, they had driven over. after school and would invariably locate me trundling home from town, our older son perched on the pram seat , our younger son tucked up and asleep inside the pram. It seemed the most natural thing in the world to hand them the door key, instruct them to go on home, let themselves in and to make a drink. I arrived to find a cheerful crowd of willing nursemaids, all dying to get their hands on the little boys!

I distinctly remember one such afternoon. It was snowy, a magical, white, quieter world that seemed as if it had slowed down. The pram acted like a snowplough, the wheels slicing through the white mounds and leaving tracks and furrows. I'm not sure whether our older son acted as an anchor or a de-stabiliser, as he shuffled around on the pram seat! We were nearly home when the girls materialised, jerking me out of my preoccupation with the surroundings. I was very grateful for this forward party who went on ahead, so that I could arrive home to find a warm house and hot drinks! In retrospect, they were such heartwarming times, making me feel quite privileged that those young women should want to be bothered with an ordinary housewife and her sometimes crying children. Maybe I was entertaining angels unawares?

The halcyon days of this era were cut short by a family crisis. My father developed a life threatening brain condition, needing radical surgery with an unknown outcome. Having hurled wet washing into a suitcase and with two small children in tow, my husband, (having to stay for work), put us on a train to face my father's uncertain future. With us relying heavily on the prayers of our Hut dwellers, he underwent a dangerous, delicate operation to try to repair the damage the condition had caused. Despite the surgeon's poor prognosis, he described his surgical result as "a miracle", managing to repair an aneurysm that was deep in the brain's cortex, the site of speech, memory, language and thought. Life was tense and exhausting. I vividly remember feeling that I could no longer go on, that it was too big to cope with. I prayed that God would send me some sign that I wasn't alone in this. The very next day, and out of this darkness came shafts of light. letters and a gift arrived from our praying friends back home, extending Rowland's Hut of unmerited love, care and comfort over the geographical distance between us. I'm reminded of the Taizé song "O Lord hear my prayer, O Lord hear my prayer. When I call, answer me". He surely did just that, simply by the timing of the mail! I've recently read that "spiritual synergy works miracles, so look for prayer partners to stand with you". Jesus said, "if two of you agree on earth concerning anything that they ask, it will be done for them by my My Father in heaven".

My father spent his first few post operative weeks on a neurological ward that exuded an atmosphere unlike any ward I'd previously experienced. It felt rather like a holy place, like the hushed silence found in a grand cathedral, its "worshippers" being in, or emerging out of, critical states of existence. There was the quiet whirring of machines, the distinct absence of banter - that usual staple component of hospital ward life. This was different - reverent, respectful but at the same time, eerie. Suddenly, there was a change of gear, progress having been such that my father was being allowed to go home to continue his long and winding road to recovery. The announcement came as a shock, a mixture of relief and dread, the relative security of hospital environment being exchanged for the unknown. The sole responsibility of looking after a post-op patient at home is a heavy coat to wear. There was going to be the need for peace and quiet, definitely not the top aim of two little boys! In any case, it was necessary to resume a more normal routine after the upside down days of hospital visiting. It was time to go home. Although I felt as though I'd been dragged through a hedge backwards, I'd been left with a sense of having come through an almost inexplicable reversal of events. Without a doubt, it was a God Happening, a God intervention, an answer to the desperate pleadings for an eleventh hour crisis. I'll never know if the surgeon who expressed his incredulity to us ever realised that in undertaking a totally unpredictable venture, he had co-operated (literally!) with the Creator.

Life should have settled down into its previous optimistic rhythm, but it refused to do so. The trauma we'd gone through caused us to decide to move back yet again to be near to my parents, deciding this time that we would sell our house first. During our previous abortive attempt to move, someone had shown interest in buying it but by then, we had decided to move back. On being informed that our property was once more for sale, the family didn't hesitate in agreeing to buy it. If we were looking for God's signposts, this was surely one of them! The plan went ahead. My husband managed to go back to the job he'd had briefly during our first attempt, we moved into a new home, and we set up camp. We went to the local church, offering our musical talents, trying to get absorbed into church life, making friends, some of them being crucial in our survival and at the same time, making ourselves available for my parents. Was I happy? In a word, no. It felt increasingly "un-right". It was like watching my life going down the drain. I was in the desert and I couldn't see any camels.

For a while, there were still remnants of Rowland's Hut, receiving visits from "Hutties" when we shared meals and filled in some of the blanks. The flavour of our new church was not totally palatable but we battled on. The music worship was helpful with songs that affected the heart. Our little boys were growing and were the source of the joy and hope we still possessed. Because my husband worked shifts, the pattern was difficult for both him and us, requiring a balancing act in maintaining family life. The sand of our desert continued to bank up, possibly higher for me at that stage than for him. My father had made an amazing recovery, but the drama his body had gone through resulted in him having slowed down. He retired from the job that, like many people, had been a huge part of his identity and purpose. However, he retained his group of friends who proved to be an emotional and social lifeline.

In the midst of the greyness, there was just one day...... There was going to be a wedding. A male Squash guy from the north was marrying a girl from the south. With a coach load travelling down, it had been arranged that we would be picked up, en-route. It suddenly felt as if we were going home. You can see that we appeared to have lost our sense of direction, both inwardly and outwardly! Dolled up and suited and booted, and with children handed over to Grandma and Grandad for a day of doting and spoiling, we stuck out our thumbs at the appointed pick up point. It was a journey reminiscent of the "Didn't we have a luverly time, the day we went to Bangor" variety, the guys n' gals of Squash and Hut . It was warm and welcoming. We felt alive and re-instated, albeit temporarily. I'm not exaggerating when I tell you that it was a hot, sunny day, full of not eastern, but northern meets southern promise, not exactly Turkish, but a delight in the wedding day sense of the word! With vows and rings exchanged, party food eaten in the informal setting of a garden, the cake cut and shared and with conversations all round, we set off into the summer evening to make the return journey. The coach and its cargo wound its slightly weary but happy way back, dropping us off at the point of departure. As we waved it off, it took with it all that overspill of both wedding and Hut delight and security but not without some of it rubbing off on us. We returned home from this joyful Christian occasion to receive a most devastating phone call. My husband's parents had returned from a holiday, also down south. After surveying the new carpeting, laid just before the holiday, and announcing that "they would be able to enjoy all this", my father-in-law felt unwell and got into bed, my mother-in-law putting it down to the day's travel. She later found him - he had suffered a fatal heart attack, her attempts to revive him having been to no avail.

The day's events lay in ashes. Our first thoughts were that we didn't drive, that it was too late for trains and that the coach we'd just left was heading in the direction of where we now needed to be. It was a total eclipse of life. Leaving my mother in law to face her night, we had to settle for making the journey next day, in order to begin the many administrative duties and arrangements that have to be done in the face of shock, pain and distress. With our children being once more taken care of by my mother and father (what a reversal of roles!) we became part of that post death pattern of activity - the arrival of my sister in law and her husband from New Zealand, the emotional visits to mortuary and funeral home, the buying of a suitable outfit for my mother in law to wear for the funeral, the many phone calls, the to-ings and fro-ings..... There was the rather "enter stage right" effect of the medication prescribed by her doctor, producing a nightly moment of drama and needing the assistance from her son and daughter as they performed an almost comedic ascent in getting her up the stairs to bed. I descended into a respiratory infection, receiving a daily infusion of "something and whisky" from my brother-in-law - no, don't ask as I didn't have a clue!

I must have recovered somewhat by the day of the funeral. I was conscripted into taking part in that most masterfully handled ritual - the preparation of the funeral tea. It was performed, and by that I mean it was a play and you were given a part, by a Greek Chorus of assorted female relatives. Plates, cutlery and tea towels were unceremoniously unearthed from forbidden places, something my mother-in-law would have gone mad about had she been aware of what was going on. It was unanimously decided that I was to be The Gopher. Believe you me, they got their money's worth! You couldn't really object and I think the accumulation of medicinal whisky helped me not to. My teenage role as one of the Three Little Maids in "The Mikado" had amply prepared me to play this adult version of subservience. Off they sent me to "the Stores" for supplies. Those of you from this corner of the country will recognise this as the colloquialism for the Co-op.

The funeral over, and with my sister in law and her husband back in New Zealand, we all had to assimilate the loss of my father-in-law. My husband also had to step up the oversight of his mother, She came to stay with us more often, but being a fiercely independent and private person, she began to pick up the threads of her life that included her love of ballroom dancing, swimming, and badminton. She continued her work as a seamstress for a sportswear company, fitting her hobbies around it but reserving the evenings for that most Holy Grail of her passion, her dancing. The life saving factor of this was the need to be with those friends who had been part of the lives of both my mother and father-in-law. Those good people became the inhabitants of her Rowland's Hut, providing support, shape, purpose and continuity. It certainly was a comfort for my husband to know she had this peg to hang her life on.

As we trudged on through the desert, a truly unexpected oasis appeared on the horizon, complete with the water and palm tree of refreshment we so desperately needed. At first it wasn't even a mirage. It was smoke and mirrors, sleight of hand, cloak and dagger - well maybe not dagger! Why did I feel at odds with myself? Why was I weary? Why did the mince I cooked for various dishes smell funny? Was it a stomach ulcer, I mused? No, not a stomach ulcer, my dear but getting nearer to the ballpark. There it was, that light bulb (for that read a hundred chandeliers) moment, that giant neon sign in the sky, that choir of angels announcement.......PREGNANT! The heaviest of pennies finally dropped, the mirage of mistaken cause rolled itself both up and away, and my brain re-entered my body.

Urged on by the midwives yelling "come on Rebecca!", (they'd decided it was a girl), our third son arrived, hopefully not with a gender crisis. He was our flesh and blood oasis, creating our trio of beautiful boys and heralding a sea change in our lives. There's a song that says "Where there is no way He makes a way" and this was the first step of the way. After the initial wobble of the seeming enormity of the task ahead and summed up in my moment of hysterical outpouring about not having enough hands(!), I adopted the technique of a juggler, learning to throw all the balls into the air and hoping they didn't land on my head! I once more entered into that routine conferred on me by a baby's needs, the one I'd always craved as a young girl and had rehearsed during my pram pushing days - other people's prams of course, containing other people's babies! I became quite adept at wrapping our youngest up in his pram, looking for all the world as if he'd been washed and dressed (he hadn't!) and depositing our other two sons at their respective school and play school, hoping they also looked like they had been washed and dressed (they had!). The little trio and I shared Rowland's Hut, created in the domestic setting of home and providing a shelter from the storm.

Despite the mounting up of my personal desert sands, there were some highly memorable characters who walked across them, leaving an indelible footprint trail in my mind. All were connected to the local Church, an amazingly diverse and resilient a bunch as you would ever wish to meet. A few are cast iron, "A" list, "A" graders as regards individuality, and they're the ones who've earned a mention my hall of memory.

Janet was made known to us through the three male students, with whom we became friends. They lived a few doors away from her, all of them attending the church we'd attached ourselves to. We got to know her at a difficult point in her life. Tony, her husband, was serving a prison sentence for trying to gas the next door neighbours for their excessive noise and constantly barking dog. It must have got under his skin to the extent that he'd fixed a gas pipe through the adjoining wall! That wasn't, by any definition, "an everyday story of country folk"! Janet was left, along with her two children, to "keep the home fires burning" (not, I hasten to add, the gas fires!). Although she was very happy flying round the local area in her car, usually at the speed of light, some kindly Church member had taken it upon himself to drive Janet to her regular prison visits. Maybe he wanted to make sure she remained in one piece, ready for the eventual homecoming. Tony's sentence finally came to an end, and he returned a duly chastened and more peaceable man, having given a whole new meaning to the cry, "It's the gas man"!

Angie was a "larger than life" young woman, with a line in "larger than life" hoop earrings, and a mainly absent husband who wasn't large in her's or their children's lives. She bounced around, all elfin haircut and moth eaten fur coat, her head bobbing as she walked, daily willing everything to hang together for her trio of girls. Being a creative person, she seemed able to make things out of nothing, and had a flair for what you could regard as either novelty or innovation, causing great amusement with the plastic flowers she "planted " in her front garden! She was resilient, operating her basic but sincere faith in God, despite the deals life handed out. Her direct but attractive personality won her friends and loyalty from the church, its members rallying round whenever she had a need that she couldn't meet. Not being one to mince words, she would announce, "Well, you'll just 'ave to 'elp me, luv", levelling this at whichever person happened to pass by! I have no doubt that the priest and the Levite in the Good Samaritan parable wouldn't have got away with it so easily! Passing by on the other side just wouldn't have been an option with Angie!

The pivotal day came when a major rescue operation had to be put in place. Our response to a phone call found Angie, her three children and the contents of her home adorning the front lawn. They had been evicted, the house having been reclaimed, owing to Angie's husband having defaulted on the mortgage - the words of the phrase "couldn't, seen and dust" was pretty accurate! It was the final straw in that particular desert and camel story, and for once, it wasn't my desert or camel! That didn't, however, count as a triumph as we surveyed this little family on the lawn, even with the surrounding plastic flowers. The glue that had kept their family life together had finally melted. A heroic effort saw Angie and the children being taken in by some kindly person, whereas the contents of the house were taken, by a chain gang of Church members, to be stored in the church hall. The council rehoused the family, but regrettably, it was several miles away. My husband and our friend Phil gathered up the house contents, and transported them to be reunited with the family. With the "wheels" once more back on their "vehicle", Angie and the girls were ready to travel along the next few miles of their life road. I hope there weren't too many hairpin bends!

The Church seemed to major in collecting its distinctive characters, Velda being one of them. She was another "larger than life" lady, in every sense of the word, with her ample proportions, bare legs, (even in the depths of winter), and always sporting a headscarf, which I regarded as her Business scarf, tied firmly under her chin. She exuded an air of mystery particularly over matters of faith, but none more so than over her house, becoming named by a local wag and subsequently referred to by one and all as "Velda Towers" (above everyone?). Somewhere along the line, there was a husband, but he remained a shadowy figure, a walk - on part in Velda's play. The children were much more prominent, both of them usually hanging onto Velda's legs, as she towered above them. Perhaps her greatest defining moment was at a certain house group meeting we attended. Upon being asked if any of us had anything to share concerning a "God" intervention that week, it was Velda who stepped into the spotlight, recounting the story of how she'd had gone up a ladder at her home but had became totally stuck. Feeling desperate, she'd apparently shouted out to God that He'd have to get her down. Was it a pair of wings, a parachute, or a knight in armour, shining or otherwise? Whether it was any of the aforementioned, or even "underpants over trousers Superman", down she'd gone, and here she was! There's a deep theological truth here, that whenever we become stuck on Life's Ladder, God will always come to our aid. As the Taizé song says, "Oh, Lord hear my prayer. When I call, answer me". He'd most certainly answered Velda's call, (which would have been loud and insistent), in bringing her safely down from her mountain top experience! Velda was indomitable in spirit, and kind in nature, and always on some street corner, knee deep in the latest neighbourhood politics, her headscarf being the daily signal that The Meeting was in progress!

Phil, John, and Rick lived together in their little rented cottage, all three of them becoming members of the local Church. Pursuing a sandwich course at the polytechnic, their shared domestic life was also strangely sandwich like, the three of them merging into a composite personality reminiscent of Zaphod Beeblebrox, the two headed character from "Hitchhikers Guide To The Galaxy", with the dubious benefit of an added extra head. They were very different in personality, driving each other (and everyone else) mad with their idiosyncrasies, the most notable one being illustrated in "the saga of John and the blue washing up bowl". He, John, insisted that the unpleasant receptacle be present at all times, and especially ready to stand to attention in the sink. Its one true value was to catch the copious amounts of cooked spaghetti attempting to be rinsed under the cold water tap, but preferring to head southwards, down the drain. Your blind eye was a useful asset when dining at Chez Madhouse! It was a case of World War Three breaking out if someone tried to wash up in the sink without the bowl being in situ. It was also possibly welcome in any place that required blue rigid plastic, becoming both a fashion accessory, or the bane of aesthetic life, depending on your view of installation art! I categorically know that the "As soon as my back is turned" school of rebellious philosophy was always implemented whenever John left the house, accompanied by whoops, whistles, balloons and the inevitable bit of muttering in dark corners.

Those corners were the harbingers of the next bone of contention, the lurking danger of Phil's bike. Its pedals were waiting to pierce you, the handlebars wanting to decapitate you, the oil from the chain hoping to decorate your best outfit, and the least bit of contact bringing the whole thing falling down on you, much like Giant Haystacks in a wrestling match on Saturday afternoon telly! If the bike didn't get you, Phil's equally giant hi-fi speakers would. The size of two football stadiums, these adorned (and I apply this loosely!) the remaining corners of the living room, not really allowing for either "living" or "room" to have any relevance to the humans who resided there, or the visitors who tried to penetrate this male stronghold.

You're possibly wondering about the third person of the trio, (or should that be trinity?). So am I, as Rick always seemed to be like that phrase, "In the third person". He really did float about in a gentle, non assertive, "I'm going to be a bumbling vicar" manner, genially nodding his head and waving his arms in non verbal assent to the hubbub that surrounded him. I seem to recall that he really was aiming to do just that - become a vicar, that is. He certainly didn't pose any kind of threat to man, beast, or butterfly, let alone the other two males of the species. One was a true Alpha male specimen, the other less so, both perpetually locking horns over matters that could have constituted a compulsive - obsessive disorder, or, in their case, an impulsive - aggressive disorder! Rick was a genial, passive, cushion-like house-mate, the other two sitting on him, figuratively speaking. He seemed happy in his own skin, whereas the Alpha male in question always seemed on the edge of "edgy", not happy in his own skin, and possibly wanting to skin not only the proverbial cat, but anyone else in his eye line.

In retrospect, the whole set up had an air of the schizophrenic, an old fashioned, "kitchen sink, washing up bowl" domesticity on the one hand, combined with a sense of the surreal on the other. Friends came for coffee, music, and spaghetti bolognese, wrestled with the bike, the speakers, and the blue bowl, and went away fed, befriended, and sometimes perplexed! The one thing the trio did do was to keep an open door for Janet and her children, who, along with my husband and I, and several other members, allowed them to "touch base", and to access our Rowland's Hut. We all kept a hand on the rudder of their lives, until Tony was decanted out of "Her Majesty's", and home once more to steer the family ship.

In addition, there were numerous others whose roles were part of this jigsaw - the lady who lived away from the area, her whereabouts a mystery, but who made her presence felt each Saturday evening by arriving at our door at precisely the same time, and always as we were trying to scoop up three children to settle them down for the night. She carried a shopping bag, rather like Roy in Coronation Street, not so much for its contents as for it being an identity badge. Maybe she was God's equivalent of the retail mystery shopper! We had no idea as to why we'd been chosen for this weekly role, but we didn't appear to have any say in the matter, it being conferred on us, even when we tried switching off the lights and hiding, the boys gagged and bound. As the Soul song says, she "just kept ringing our bell"! I don't know to this day what the private purpose was, but having just listened to a talk on the topic of things God drops into our lives that are seemingly inexplicable, I feel chastened, and hope I was more gracious than I felt I was!

I realise that in trawling through my memories of events, there was a parallel to a situation experienced in another time and place. It was that of the young females who attached themselves to our little boys. Lovely Linda, another Church member and neighbour of Janet, came on the scene at the time of our third son's birth, offering to take him out in his pram for a walk, initially in between feeds and as he grew, as a little shopping companion. He was a placid and sleepy baby, very rarely awake on my journeys to deposit and collect the older two from school and play school. He was a little mound under his soft white covers, other mums wondering if he was actually there! However, all apparently changed when Linda wheeled him out of sight - and thankfully, out of earshot. According to several sightings, he would bawl lustily and incessantly all the way there and back to Linda's chosen destination. She would be doing her best to look cool and classy in her carefully chosen pram wheeling ensemble (she was quite a fashionista in those days), and I would have done my best in making him look cool and classy with his best outfit and pram quilt. I expect he served two purposes, in both bringing out her maternal feelings, and also in being her little fashion accessory too! I must say that she never seemed flustered, and always returned happy and fulfilled, just like the little mum I hoped she'd finally become.

Margaret, the student daughter of Church members, asked permission to work with our baby son for her college child study. Having used my little cousin for my own college child study, and knowing how important it was, I readily agreed. Our little son's social life was expanding, with Linda by day, and now Margaret before tea for baths, play and chat. My one regret from this time was in not having asked for a copy of the tapes she recorded of him complaining and reacting in his little croaky voice at being undressed for his bath, Margaret chatting to him as she encouraged him to splash about. I would be downstairs making tea and keeping an eye on my other two boys, and at the same time, straining to hear and interpret the sounds from above, resisting the urge to wade in and calm him down. I hope he gave Margaret a lot of pleasure as she gathered the material for her profile and that she scored highly. I also hope that somewhere inside, my son retained a memory of all the love and attention that young girl gave him. I certainly have!

During this more settled time, we'd started going to a fairly local Baptist church where we began to be built up again. I even managed to re-enter the world of teaching, egged on by my teacher neighbour. She had temporarily stepped outside her role as Mum to small children, and had been press ganged by a rather desperate primary Head to do some supply teaching. My neighbour used the same technique on me, resulting in it propelling me out of my cosy reverie and pitching me into the cut and thrust of the same school. It was very cut and totally thrust! I admit to having enjoyed the challenge, but doubt I did much more than lion tame, it being a tough social environment on which to cut my post-mum teeth! The pay was the real incentive, affording new carpeting and a holiday but in retrospect, I asked myself whether it had been worth all the physical exertion and military precision. However, there was a positive. Our two older sons were now at school and our youngest became my father's little daytime companion. He was grafted into his Grandad's social events, including the regular coffee gatherings in the city where I'm sure he would have been the centre of attention. Without a doubt, it enriched my father's life after the trauma of his life changing illness, at the same time benefiting our youngest son from the quality time he was given. Despite all this, there was still the feeling that we were not in the right place. I never ceased the daily prayer to be released from what felt like a prison, the bars being the unhappy memories of all that had seemed to go wrong or was unfulfilled in that desert place. As Steve Chalke said - and probably others too, "It's Friday, but Sunday's coming". Then it happened! The door swung open and we could see the exit sign! The application for a job with a northern insurance firm resulted in my husband being offered it. We had been handed "the golden ticket to Willie Wonka's chocolate factory", "the three bananas of the fruit machine" win, "the Get out of prison" Monopoly card. There was a visceral certainty that the Way had been provided.

The selling of the house was not without its challenges. With uncanny timing, our house and the adjoining one went up for sale at one and the same time, viewers obviously comparing and contrasting both. I still remember the Saturday afternoon when everything seemed to happen in slow motion. A couple, having been next door were making their way up our path. They viewed, they went away to deliberate, they chose, they un-chose us and thought they might choose next door....They were toying with us, much like a cat with an unfortunate mouse. I called "Time" on my uncertainty and decided to wash my hands of them and to hope for some more viewers. What a result! Against the odds, they decided it was our house they wanted. I had gone way beyond the swinging from the rafters stage, wondering if we would actually get to the end of the transaction with such an ambivalent couple. We took the opposite strategy in choosing our new house - a one day flying visit where we viewed three houses from the outside and only one internally. Fitting our criteria, we chose it. "Simples", as the television meerkat ad says! My husband became the advance party for our move in having to go ahead to start his job, staying in a bed and breakfast during the week and coming back at weekend, I commanded events chez nous, including cleaning up the act for moving and the sorting, throwing way and packing requisite for such an occasion. After six weeks of that regime, I have every admiration for single parents who perform their job with such heroism. Our trusty solicitor managed to conceal the legal setback that had threatened to derail the whole move - something to do with conveyancing law in Scotland, the country from which our purchasers were moving. As our friend says, hey ho!

We moved into our new home on a mellow September morning. It felt like we were taking the lid off a new and exciting gift. The house immediately took on the character of a furniture factory, my husband having to tackle boxes of flat pack wardrobes and drawers, as all in the old house were built in! We became acquainted with the idiosyncrasies of the property, our two sons started their new school and our youngest his play school. God had left His calling card with my husband through an encounter with some members of a local Baptist church who were involved in a tent crusade. Strolling on the sea front one evening, my husband talked to one of the members and gathered the relevant information about the church. It didn't end there. A few days after moving in, it was the turn of the Jehovah's Witnesses. I think the word had gone round that we were in town! On their departure, I managed to crash the still unfamiliar up and over garage door down on my head. It didn't appear to augur well.

I hardly had time to examine the crater in my skull before the door bell rang. This, by the way, was the front door - we were still getting used to the position of the doors! Dave and Nikki, the husband wife pair who came through our door, were to be significant in our lives. They also went to the Baptist church and were calling because Jean, our new next door neighbour had told Nikki, her friend, that she thought we read the Bible ......! As David Helfgott said, "It's a mystery". There was a further revelation from Dave that added to our sense of being drawn to this church. He announced he was a bass guitarist.....drum roll, that he played in the worship band....louder drum roll (and of interest to my guitarist husband) and then the proverbial Big One.... He used to belong to Canaan, the Christian band.....and the drum rolled and fell over. We narrowly avoided falling down and bowing, such had the impact been on our musical lives. Hadn't we gone to the Albert Hall and the back of beyond to see them in concert? Hadn't they appeared with Cliff Richard, Larry Norman, Millstone Grit, Gordon Giltrap, Trinity Folk? Hadn't we made all those Concert visits with our Rowland's Hut friends? A living legend was now sitting in our new lounge, and we were sitting at his feet, my enthusiasm for this church rising. However, there was the wardrobe building programme, having brought with us several flat-packs that needed assembling, so we reluctantly had to put our first visit on ice. As Nikki wryly observed, "It'll still be there next week" and departed. We later discovered that she was en-route to run her Boys Brigade group, one of the many active passions of her life, and through which she'd done great things for those boys who'd passed through its doors. The cherry on the cake was a phone call from the pastor, apologising for not being able to come and see us but welcoming us to the area and church. So, more calling cards from the God who cared, delivered by those whose hearts had been given a heavenly nudge.

We went, we saw and we conquered. The pastor was engaging, the atmosphere intentional and the congregation an intriguing mix. Here would be a Hut, a refuge, a holy space - not perfect but a living place and a place in which to live. My mind took a snapshot, a picture to be taken out and studied at leisure. It was immediately evident that the man at the helm of this church possessed both a heart and an intellect, both qualities desirable for effective pastoring. As I let the effect of this person wash over me, I felt that he was displaying the hallmarks of Jesus in a way that affected me. My overriding impression was of a man who had a respect for those in front of him, with an integrity of spirit that appealed on both the personal and corporate levels. My definition of him is that he didn't make you go spiritually where he may have been but where you felt you couldn't. We were once more going to be able to dwell in Rowland's Hut.

They were kaleidoscopic days, when all the pieces of our lives were rotated to produce new patterns. Our latent musical talents were recovered and used in the arena of worship, the prevalent Vineyard style suiting our folk background and my husband's ability to roll one song into another. It was an attractive, gentle and more democratic style than is being offered today. More importantly, the songs spoke Scripture to people's hearts and spirits, something that could be carried around to be drawn on in times of need, as well as in times of plenty! The pastor conferred on us the role of house group leadership, a role that had its practical challenges in a house with three young boys! My husband masterminded the worship and I undertook the teaching element but I'm not guaranteeing my success in that area! I did, however enjoy it immensely.

It was a role that required flexibility and also the skills of negotiator, diplomat and counsellor! We were certainly put to the test over one of our young couples, with their "on-off" relationship. A typical house group evening would be as follows: Ring ring (phone) - "Is M coming tonight?" Depending on answer given, the response would be, "Well, I'll come then" or "I'm not coming then". So far, so delicate! Ten minutes later: Ring ring (phone) - "Is N coming tonight?". Depending on answer given, the response would be the same. Each house group night took on the nature of a tennis match, the "balls" travelling down the phone line with deadly accuracy, resulting in a constant score of deuce! Their courting ritual was colourful, to say the least, the tension as taut as any Wimbledon racket! Their marriage continued in much the same vein. After declaring undying love and apologies to his bride at their wedding reception, the game resumed, and after a child and a move to another continent, they separated and divorced. End of story? Not at all. They are now happily reconciled, remarried and remoulded - older, wiser and no longer playing tennis, as it were!

Our much loved pastor was only on loan. After a few short years, he was poached from our midst by the august theological powerhouse that has trained countless Baptist ministers of the Faith. After a patch of to-ing and fro-ing that strangely resembled our own north-south meanderings, he rose up the ranks to become the captain of the aforesaid ship, exampling to the earnest acolytes the grace and rigour needed to steer their own future ships of faith. He left behind him a rich legacy of books, his collective wisdom encapsulated in pages that bear those same hallmarks we recognised in him on that sunny September morning. The passage of time saw our relationship with this place not exactly severed, but weakened. We found ourselves becoming hippy-like in our decision to drop out. There were reasons, which in retrospect, were relatively unimportant. We should have perhaps persevered more, possibly having made a mountain out of a molehill. There is a price to pay in becoming divorced from your church fellowship, every bit as painful as divorce in marriage. At the time of writing, we are attending a large community church. It's a different millennium, a different culture and a different worship style, the attendant characteristics presenting its different challenges. However, despite the turning of the spiritual tide, God hangs onto us and we try to hang onto him.

It seemed unbelievable that Ruth, the spiritual Mum of the Squash, was going to be eighty. In honour of this auspicious occasion, there was to be a celebration, and we had been invited to what was a wonderful assembly of family and friends sharing a superb lunch, seeing Rowland's Hut once more working its relational magic. It popped up through the crowd and encapsulated the Hut dwellers of the past, a "same but different" experience that happens with the passing of time. Fragments of memories surfaced and were exchanged, a bit like a child filling in a colouring book. The judicious seating arrangements meant that we found ourselves grouped with "Hutties", ideal for rekindling friendships. Some of them have built into strong and essential relationships, some providing support and enabling shared Christian service. Dave and Jan have been instrumental in these, generating opportunities for leading church worship in music and word. The four of us, together with Paul and Grace pooled our strengths and hopefully injected a sense of God's presence in small rural gatherings. I certainly felt He was very kind in that He was unearthing our hidden talents and renewing our sense of worth that had become submerged under the cares of life. We had all caught up with each other further along the road, battle worn but still walking.

It's with sadness that we remember those no longer here, those in the heavenly roll call of honour - Rowland, John, Wesley, Ken, Brian, Andrew - all thought of with love and affection and missed - so missed. God holds them in His heart and we hold them in our hearts, waiting for the day we shall all meet on that "Other Shore" - the one mentioned in the bidding prayer of the Radio Four Christmas Eve Carols from Kings service. It's the shore of eternity, the meeting place of all those saints gone before and to whom we'll be added. It helps to talk in such poetic terms about the leaving and joining we all have to face. At least, it helps me and, I suspect, others like me. The journey we'll have to take Toward The Unknown Region (Ralph Vaughan Williams) is unknowable in human terms but we know The Tour Guide who will see us safely there, the One who said He wouldn't leave or abandon us.

Chapter 6: The Rose Of Sharon

"The desert and the parched land will be glad; the wilderness will rejoice and blossom."
- Isaiah 35 v. 1

It was like a woodpecker hammering away at my brain. Get in touch with Paul and Grace. Get in touch. Peck, peck, peck, an insistent, persistent voice refusing to go away. It was Christmas Eve. There had been thirty something Christmas Eves since we'd last shared more than the exchange of Christmas cards or as my mother would have said, "A Communiqué", the capital letters in her voice denoting a matter of grave importance! I finally gave in to text appeal and sent one. There was shared surprise and joy over the re-establishment of our friendship and promises made to meet in the near future. The season came and went and the normal rhythm of life resumed. However, my husband and I were under mounting pressure from a situation whose lid we were just about managing to keep on.

A close personal friend was living with us at the time. He had not found life easy, depression making it hard to make the best choices, and draining him of confidence. It was becoming obvious that as his ability to cope with life was decreasing, his drinking was increasing. He was still managing to hold down his job by day, disappearing to drink by night. We were aware that we were out of our depth, but feeling committed to see this through, we ploughed on, head down with what faith we could muster. I kept hold of the irrational but single minded conviction that like

Superman, God would come and perform a rescue job. We pushed every button we could think of, sharing our worries with friends both inside and outside the Christian community, wanting and willing our friend to find release. There didn't appear to be any light at the end of an increasingly dark tunnel for him or for us. My mobile phone's screen-saver is a picture of two slender trees standing closely together. They are clinging to the side of a windswept hill with nothing else in sight. However, they are rooted in green grass, speaking of sustenance and life, very much as we were doing.

It was around this time that we received an invitation to visit Paul and Grace, and to spend the day with them on "The Rose Of Sharon", the place that had become their home. To those with biblical knowledge, it evokes the image of the desert that is filled with those blossoming flowers. Do you know, that's just what had happened! Paul and Grace having emerged from their own particular desert that included the falling apart of their respective marriages and church life. Paul had been the pastor of an independent church, but upon the suggestion to his members that they become a fellowship that operates on a seven day basis, was called to account before the committee. The question asked of him was, "Who do you think you are, Moses?" ..... Paul's response was "in that case, next Sunday will be my last as pastor". Exit Paul! Followed by the collapse of his marriage and leaving the family home, he found himself in a very dark place, something we would have known about had we'd been more in touch.

He spent a devastating time living in a flat, experiencing a season of bleak and separating loneliness. For Grace, it had been a bit of a last resort, her slender means allowing her to secure a small narrow boat. The ensuing relationship between Paul and Grace led to marriage, and consequently the "Rose of Sharon" became their new marital home, a place of shelter, sanctuary and strength. This description contains the seeds of Rowland's Hut - a tower of refuge, a balm of healing, which is a reference to the plant found in Gilead in the Bible. They certainly needed this, finding themselves ostracised from church and community life, and suffering strain in their family relationships. Life on the canal afforded them a haven, a place of tranquillity and calm, firstly for themselves and then for all the bruised and battered souls who came the way of "The Rose", finding love, acceptance and healing.

Paul and Grace are creative people, Paul being a guitarist, songwriter, artist and writer of books and Grace a maker of all things creative. Together, they are puppeteers, making their own puppets and writing their own scripts. They have served communities of needy children and their parents well, with their Christmas shows and many parties. They use their musical gifts to serve God in services and gatherings and lend an listening ear and soft heart to those within their sphere of influence. They moved from being capsized by their first marriages to the affirming environment of "The Rose", emerging from the bottom of their ocean to the sparkling surface where they have rediscovered their value, before both God and Man.

The day appointed for our visit finally came. Sitting in a garden centre cafe, it wasn't long before cards were in the table, cats came out of bags, and beans were spilled - metaphorically, that is! We felt able to share honestly with Paul and Grace, and our story was received with gentleness and respect. We hope we received their story as graciously. The day on "The Rose" saw us sharing at a deep and often tearful (Paul!) level. Having grasped the seriousness of our situation with our friend, we revealed the height of our problems, the effect being that of standing at the feet of the high peaks of a mountain range! Little did we appreciate the pivotal nature of this day, this "three in a row and a bonus day". Our farewells were said and home we went to resume wading in the muddy waters of our existence. We weren't to know that God was about to build a bridge over those particular waters. Our texting resumed and the weeks continued to roll, if not to rock.

My husband's sister and her husband arrived from Australia. We were to celebrate my mother in law's ninetieth birthday, managing to do this in spite of her increasingly fragile mental health and followed by her hospitalisation and subsequent admittance to a care home. At the same time, we had cause to rejoice over the birth of our first beautiful grandson, travelling between two hospitals to visit a newborn and a ninety year old! A few short months later saw the arrival of our first beautiful granddaughter, bringing a sense of renewal and joy to our ravaged lives. Added to this mix was the need for my mother to have a cataract procedure! We really didn't have enough hands with which to handle this problem, so drafted in the welcome but temporary help of an aunt. I should mention here that my mum's mental health was also compromised, necessitating help and support on all levels.

With hindsight, I realise that God had already launched the lifeboat, and was making plans for the rescue. Paul and I are people of words, so texting soon became a necessary tool and a lifeline of hope and support in the few short weeks of our reconnection. Alongside were a friend and her husband who take

God at his word and prayed for our situation, texting messages of support. These good people erected scaffolding around our tottering state, preventing us from utterly collapsing. All attempts to search Yellow Pages for counsellors and addictions left me feeling it wasn't the way. Leading a horse to water doesn't always result in getting it to drink. After all, we couldn't make our friend agree to talk to somebody. So on we went.

Then it happened - a shaft of light, a ray of hope, a sense of Someone with us in the tunnel.... Paul had woken in the night with a clear plan of action for our friend. He knew he had to write him a letter, not in entirety but in fifteen portions and starting with one sentence. Each subsequent letter would have an added sentence so that there would be a complete letter by number fifteen. It was a brilliant concept, ensuring that anything missed in discarded letters would be present in each successive one. Paul had instructed us to leave the day's delivered letter on the table for our friend to pick up and not to say anything. What a clever idea for someone who wouldn't and couldn't talk about himself! Paul asked us to carefully and prayerfully consider whether we were in agreement with it. I have to admit that it challenged me to my roots! After waiting for deliverance, it made me feel distinctly wobbly. How could I let this happen to our friend who was in such bad shape? I felt I would be responsible for such an "odd" scheme and worried about the repercussions. I submitted to having to rely upon my husband's decision in this instance as I couldn't trust my own. He thought it was exactly right in trusting Paul and his relationship with God. Paul had a history of perceiving God in ways that others do not.

The letters began to arrive. All we were required to do was to pick them up off the mat and leave them on the kitchen table. It happened wordlessly, silently, an act that seemed almost clandestine. A sign that God is the author of humour was reflected in the fact that there was a postal strike in action, the result being that the orderly design of each numbered letter was disrupted, a gap between some, several arriving together. Maybe this fitted in with our friend's drinking pattern and mood! I noted that some letters had been screwed up and thrown in the bin but THE PLAN had taken this into account. The day of the fifteenth and final letter dawned, preceded by two epically worrying days. Our friend had not come home. A phone call from his boss added to the anxiety, informing us that she'd received a phone call to say that he'd had his drinks spiked and he'd been "out of it" on the floor.

Our friend and the fifteenth letter arrived on our mat at the same time. He took to his bed even though it was morning and he was supposed to go to work. We had been invited away for the weekend with several other Christians so went out to buy our share of supplies. We had been grateful for the invite but it was becoming less of a possibility. Also, what now after the letters? On returning home with our shopping, we realised our friend hadn't gone to work. His door was firmly closed. It was at this point that my husband could no longer cope with it, leaving it to me to face what was behind the door. It was patently obvious that work was not an option and that we were facing an "eleventh hour" situation. I found myself saying to our friend that he needed to be in hospital, his reply being "okay"..... I was immediately galvanised into action and ran down to phone the weekend duty doctor. His reply was not to wait for him as it would be several hours before he could get to our friend but to take him to hospital and to ask for mental health services. Do you know how hard it is for a five foot, one inch female to handle a spaced out, nearly six foot male, to try to pull suitable clothes on him and haul him downstairs and into a taxi? No, I didn't until that day! God must have given me a double portion of galvanisation! In the middle of this, our friends called to collect us, but ended up collecting just the food. It all seemed like a dream - or more to the point, a nightmare but somehow we got there and the waters began to part. Thank goodness for the allotted, no nonsense Irish counsellor who parked us in a room and took our friend off. We sat in a trance, everything around us seeming remote and irrelevant. Meanwhile, the counsellor was jerking our friend's mind into making decisions to take responsibility for his life, telling him that if he carried on in the same way, he wouldn't have one.

He was discharged on the condition that he would attend the alcohol abuse centre on Monday morning and go back to work. Exhausted and disoriented from the day's events, we crawled home to try to make sense of it all. I managed to create a much needed meal, our friend not having eaten since I don't know when. He flopped into bed with promises of going to the centre and also to make a doctor's appointment to address his depression, this surely being the crux of the problem. Wow, progress indeed and a very brave admission! My husband remained understandably unconvinced but I couldn't raise the White Flag now. The next day was Sunday and I clung desperately to both our friend's, and God's, promises. Sleep was in short supply but somehow Monday materialised, and with it, the hopes and fears for the future.

You no doubt want to know the outcome. Did our friend keep his promises? To paraphrase Bob The Builder, Yes. He Did!!! With a new resolve, he got up early and made the journey to the centre, where he was assigned a female support worker. He then saw his doctor who prescribed medication and who saw him on a regular basis. His support worker had a profound effect on him and he had great respect for her. She was able to empathise, uncovering his intelligence and academic standing and even suggested he would be an ideal candidate for training as a mental health counsellor. As she helped him with his own mental health and previous addiction, we helped him to become physically healthier. He'd lost lots of weight and needed building up. He needed to do regular walking to soak up the tension of withdrawal, at the same time fighting bouts of tiredness, lethargy and depression. We were only too happy to give our friend everything he needed as he used his determination to get well. We could hardly believe what was happening but were thankful to God for His amazing rescue operation. We hope that he felt secure as we placed Rowland's Hut over the ashes of our lives. We could all take shelter, as the rebuilding process began.

I wonder what you make of it all - the inner woodpecker insistence, the plan, the letters, the events leading up to the day our world changed? I can hardly believe that this actually happened to us all. It's like looking down the wrong end of binoculars! Looking at our friend's life now - an upwardly mobile manager for an international chain and now living independently, we can't ignore the transformation. We can't underestimate Paul's obedience in offering God's escape route. I can't forget my husband's single-minded willingness to endorse it. In re-visiting this true story, we see the love and compassion of our God at work in the world today. As for Paul and Grace, they continue to offer their lives for God's purposes. They now live on dry land, having swapped their floating pencil case (Paul's words) for a lovely house. It wasn't the one of their imagination but the one that supplied all their needs and more. They'll be the first to admit that their minds had to be well and truly changed!

This has been a chapter about seasons of life. I recently rediscovered a little article once sent by Paul and it seems fitting to include it here:-

A story..........
A man had four sons. He wanted them to judge things carefully, so he sent each on a quest to look at a pear tree far away. The first son went in the Winter, the second in Spring, the third in Summer and the fourth in the Autumn.
After they returned home, he asked them to describe what they had seen. The first son said the tree was ugly and twisted. The second son said it was covered in green buds and full of promise. The third reported it was filled with sweet fragrant blossoms. The last son disagreed with all of them and said it was heavy with ripe fruit.
The father pointed out they were all correct for they had each seen just one season of the tree's life. He explained that we cannot judge people or circumstances until all the pieces are available to present a complete picture.
Remember, don't give up when it's Winter, for you will miss the promise of Spring, the beauty of Summer and the fulfilment of Autumn.

After due consideration, I felt that the closing words should be those given to Paul. It's God's love letter to our friend, an arrow piercing the darkness, a strong arm of rescue. It's universal, and it's for you and me!

Dear ....

Do you know you are special?

Do you know you are unique?

Do you know you were put on this earth for a purpose? A plan which is absolutely designed with you in mind?

Do you know that there is someone who knows ABSOLUTELY what you have been through and are going through right now?

Do you know that there is someone who is willing to help you through thick and thin , whatever men may think of you, however men may judge you?

The question is........ARE you willing to receive that help?

The truth is, man is allotted a very little short time on this earth............

and every minute is one less of his life span!

Time is TOO precious to waste, as a "yesterday" wasted can never be retrieved.

I want you to know that, if you really want it, my help is available 24/7 I have been trying to help you for a LONG time, but you also have to be willing to be helped.

NO-ONE can take responsibility for YOUR life...ONLY YOU!

PLEASE don't reject my help.......YOU'RE BIGGER THAN THAT.............

You need to renew your mind, you need a change of heart, you and ONLY you can allow me to put you on the right course.............

IT'S YOUR CHOICE, but don't put it off! Life is TOO short to waste it.

From Jesus, with LOVE.

Chapter 7: Who Writes The Songs?

"He put a new song in my mouth, a hymn of praise to our God."
- Psalm 40 v.3

As my life has progressed through all the various musical incarnations, I have come to accept that culture today seems to dictate as much, if not more than ever, the style that has deeply affected our musical worship style. It has to be said that as a rule of thumb, beauty and dare I say, lyricism are at a premium in the current song style. "The beat" seems to be the driving force and more recently, words are being replaced by Whoaas! Now, please don't think I've swallowed the whole dish of sour grapes. Coming from a line of Jewish Show Boys with a song and dance background, music has always been an essential component of my existence, my twelve year old self once exclaiming that God WAS music! As the old song says, "All I want is loving you and music, music, music". My theology at that tender age was obviously of the gut reaction type, but I would like to think it's now more informed, but visceral nonetheless!

Never has there been such a hot potato in our church gatherings as that of music worship. Or on closer inspection, maybe there has been and it's never cooled down. The arena of spiritual expression through music has been littered with casualties - plainsong in, plainsong out. West Gallery in, West Gallery out. Organs in, organs - well, you know the rest. It's been a case of the musical Hokey Cokey all the way! Music has been used to express, impress and depress! It's such a subjective area and can be either wondrous or an obstructive hindrance. We all tend to become conditioned by the worship practices and expressions of our particular faith route. We can be found bowing, genuflecting, kneeling, smiling, shaking, crying, clapping, arm waving, hand thrusting, swaying and swinging - with or without chandeliers! There are invisible lines that we don't or mustn't cross, stuff that makes us cross and sometimes worship that, quite frankly, makes us cross eyed. If you, like me are exposed to worship "where the beat goes on", you have my sympathy! After all, it's an advantage if "the beat" eases up occasionally in order to let the nervous system recover! I know that "one man's ceiling is another man's floor" but does the floor remain still enough to stand on when others are using it as a springboard to the ceiling?

It is necessary at this point to establish that there's no such thing as Christian music, only Christian words. The marrying of certain music styles and words produces a climate that is evocative, the dictionary definition of evocative being that of "bringing strong images, memories and feelings to mind". The combination of music and Christian words allow God to make His presence felt more closely - or not, as the case may be! In answer to the comment that God's not deaf, I want to yell that if He had any sense, He wouldn't be here anyway! In addressing the noise level problem, it gives a whole new meaning to the term "sound bites". Being facetious is a safety valve but here's a sobering thought. A passage in the Message version of the Bible states "Don't be flip with the sacred. Banter and silliness give no honour to God. Don't reduce holy mysteries to slogans. In trying to be relevant, you're only being cute and inviting sacrilege". Musicians and worshippers offer each other a holy space in which God can be sensed in a closer way, both personally and corporately.

There's a huge responsibility in the art of being a "worship leader", as today's parlance has it. There's the practical aspect of songs actually being singable, combined with the spiritual temperature of the worshippers and whether the needs of those are being attempted to be met. One tendency for those leading is to lose the awareness of the worshippers and their needs and to drift off into their own worship space. Another is to use the time to generate as much "white noise" as is humanly possible in the confines of small premises. I'm with St. Paul on this one, all things being permissible but not always wise. In other words, don't be barmy in what we inflict on each other in the name of worship! We need to respect what he called the weaker brother, by serving a mixed diet of songs instead of a plate containing only carrots!

We need to unashamedly mention the factor of age. If our worship life is going to be based solely on the rock concert model, we're really alienating the all-age aspect of being Church. After watching wall-to-wall broadcasts of worship concerts, with its arenas full of young people, I have to admit that it's brilliant on one level, but pointedly selective on the other. However, it makes me wonder if there are arrowed signs in the foyers, directing those of certain ages by stating, "This way to the Polyester Room"! Is this a case of out of sight, out of mind?

A recent addition to the worship experience is "the countdown" on the screen, encouraging worshippers to assemble, much like the more formal bidding prayer. Perhaps a more bizarre addition is the use of the smoke machine, creating a night club atmosphere for those who now pogo to the beat. Imagination can just about equate this to the all pervading incense favoured by some but shunned by the less exotically inclined. I have had the dubious pleasure to sample this form of worship for myself. Herded into a tightly packed and dimly lit room, the feeling was one of rising claustrophobia. The incessant beat and incongruous swirling smoke, together with the rise and fall of the pogo dance made for a highly charged scenario with no obvious way of escape. The people, seemingly happy and shiny, rose and fell to the beat as one man, their exuberance filling the room, their body language claiming every bit of space and every breath of air that we more passive and perplexed worshippers needed. In defence of the overkill attitude, the church community was on its final day of an in-house conference, headlined by an internationally renowned speaker, and the reason for our visit. All had reached the pinnacle of enthusiasm and motivation. It was like being trapped in a room with airtight windows and doors, but with no means of escaping. I wouldn't like to give the impression that they weren't "walking the walk" and "talking the talk". They were! It can best be described as wearing different styles of spiritual "shoes and clothes" for their journey than the ones worn by others, maybe more disco than heavy duty. Either way, it was a tough call to try to be assimilated into this environment and more to the point, to match up the speaker in this surreal situation to the realism and acerbic wit of his books and devotional aids. It has to be said that there seemed to be discrepancies but it could have been the "feet of clay" factor.

There's nothing like coming face to face with a hero whom you've perhaps revered from afar! Appearing before you, the mystery falls away, the giant of imagination shrinks, and all stature and intrigue is stripped away. It's a sobering moment when you have to invest your faith in someone whose integrity you find yourself having to re examine. I'm sure that seeing the fallen hero in that particular environment didn't help. It reduced his credibility rating, albeit temporarily, the gap between written word and microphone puzzlingly wide. It definitely wasn't a Rowland's Hut encounter of the third or any kind! I don't want to give you the impression that the community isn't valid in its aims and out workings. It's vibrant, passionate and committed to Kingdom values and is kind and generous to all in its path. Perhaps it's "grumpy old woman" syndrome so I must bear that in mind when bringing down my heavy hammer of judgement. Maybe it was the shock of arriving on what outwardly seemed like Planet Loony. Possibly it was aesthetic and social distaste. Definitely it was being surrounded by bodies being too "close up and personal", pulsating, gyrating and consuming my ever decreasing space. I went to worship God but found myself in a combat zone, an "I'm not a celebrity but PLEASE get me out of here" nightmare. It was a case of another day, another dollar as our transatlantic cousins intone. Exiting into the beautiful midday sunshine, I went through a process of decompression, reminiscent of the one undertaken by deep sea divers. It also felt strangely akin to the readjustment needed after sitting in a cinema, exchanging my willing suspension of disbelief for my more normal(?) brain activity. In this instance, the suspension hadn't been all that willing!

You may be heartened to hear that I have since reviewed my vast disappointment in my fallen hero. I have managed to reinstate him on his wobbly plinth! Now that the event has shrunk into the distant past, I can once more embrace his life observations and admonitions in the manner they are offered, relying on them to illustrate, illuminate and confirm that we're on this journey together. I can go past the community building with impunity and without feeling retributive. What a difference a day makes -

or in this instance, a few hundred! I wish I were more like a chameleon, changing colour at the drop of a hat so that I could happily merge in to any situation. Not being one means I have to be less condemning when I'm faced with that which feels foreign and alien to my belief structure and sensibilities. How noble it all sounds! How I repeatedly fail when challenged! I ask myself why, as humans, we are locked up with our own internal road map and find it hard to be prepared to take someone else's B road instead of the M something of our preconceptions. It's worse when we do this with God, receiving collateral damage from banging into proverbial brick walls by insisting we'll "do it our way". We should go as far as we can in finding and accepting points of unity with fellow believers, both in and out of given worship groupings. This, however does not always constitute that special, God given bonding that occurs in Rowland's Hut. You cannot replicate a formula or pattern of behaviour. You cannot pretend or urge, demand or expect. It just happens, a time, place and people thing. It's a gift from God, a place to be, to breathe, to accept yourself, to actually like yourself and to be liked. It's a place to value and to be valued, to appreciate and to be appreciated, to love and be loved. It's where God can love you and ask you to be your best in giving your gifts and talents. Wow, that sounds like a big claim and at the same time, a taste of The Kingdom! When do we ever find all these eggs in one basket? If we do, when we do, hang onto them - and the basket!

My reason for the title being called "Who Writes The Songs" is to uncover the God who brought Creation into being. It's also to examine the nature He originally gave us but was then determined by the actions of our original parents, Adam and Eve. It makes us look at the way we choose to express His existence, through music, word and attitude. It indicates a God who knows that we veer off course in our stubbornness, sometimes thinking that anything goes and bowing too easily to popular culture with its pluses and minuses, its strengths and shortcomings. It makes us think about our blind spots, and how we insist on delivering what we think will please people and keep them in church, often providing the lowest common denominator and demeaning the whole act of worship. If we take the time to look round during our times of worship, we can see those who cannot engage owing to the inappropriate choice of material. I know you can't please all of the people all of the time, but it is insufficient and offensive to make worshippers the problem, having personally been told that perhaps I should go elsewhere to worship...?

If we're not careful, our churches can become like the Humpty Dumpty of the nursery rhyme. We join, sit on the "wall" together in our walk and worship, then an element such as the style of worship imposed upon us starts to eat into us. We become destabilised, leading to "a great fall". As with the nursery rhyme where "All the King's horses and all the King's men, couldn't put Humpty together again", we sometimes never recover sufficiently enough to trust ourselves to another group of believers, leaving us feeling and acting separated from the Body that should be helping to sustain our faith walk. There is a lot of fragmentation and collateral damage resulting from this type of imposition. The refusal to both be listened to by leaders, and to listen to each other in exploring how we can corporately express our faith, diminishes our value and input as God's people.

This, of course, brings into question the role and validity of the Body. God reaches us through our souls, the God-given essence of our beings. If we discern Him in our inner beings, we should surely be able to articulate our needs and feelings arising out of these encounters. Whereas we don't have the right to dictate the ways of our church, we are able to share and suggest better ways of serving and being. We shouldn't be surprised but dismayed when people give up, down tools and walk off the job of Kingdom building. We shouldn't lord it over each other in matters that cause dissatisfaction. We shouldn't sweep things under already dusty carpets and we shouldn't easily send people from our presence as though they were naughty schoolchildren. I acknowledge the valuable and God given role of the worship leader, I myself having been one. It shouldn't mean that it's a watertight role without input, suggestion or question from others. The role is NOT that of ego on legs but one of facilitating worshippers to come closer into God's presence. It carries with it all the responsibility of the Old Testament Levites, whose job as priests was to lead the worshippers. They headed the procession, their banners raised in acknowledgement of the God they were worshipping. The role requires sensitivity, awareness of those worshipping, and a sense of the needs of the day.

The worshipping community isn't there to suit the needs of the musicians but rather the reverse. It really is a spiritual gift to sense the mind of God and His people. It's not a perfect science, or art but it's a living thing. It's where God likes to dwell on the throne we build through our worship. Sometimes it's the difference between a drive-in fast food outlet and a classy restaurant. The former requires us to grab the food in a disposable container and proceed to eat on the run. The latter affords a leisurely, more elegant and lingering meal in a classy restaurant where the customer is king. God's our King, so let's look to the way we honour that, and let's not presume that one size fits all. In feeding people a musical diet solely based on popular styles, let's not assume that it is necessarily spiritually nutritious. This can be an easy option, based on what people are used to in their everyday lives, and possibly attracting people for the wrong reasons. Even if they're there for the right reasons, there can be limitations in where they can journey in worship. Let's make sure we're not short-changing people, and stunting their spirits.

Music is such a beautiful, mind blowing gift and it's sad when we relegate its place to a bit of hand clapping, foot stamping and heavy duty body popping. It's not necessarily wrong but it's only half the story. I like nothing more than to be in a tent with three thousand worshippers, most (not all) pouring out praise and trying to raise the roof of the tent - that's if the pounding rain doesn't get there first! However, we need to allow ourselves to be led to a quieter, deeper, centred place where God can tenderise our battered souls and apply His ointment. It's being led "beside the still waters" where we can find restoration or just to stand still for a while to allow God to see our wounds. I'm just imagining all of us standing or sitting in a worship time. As we begin to warm to the sense of God coming nearer, He's surveying the wreckage of the car crash effect of our inner selves, and longing to start the mending process. He can see the areas that we have made "no-go" zones, the places of shame, of despair, of rebellion, of hopelessness. He needs to be able make contact. You can see clearly that it's hard to hear Him in a high driving, up tempo, turbo charged climate - not impossible, but hard. We give to Him when we praise but He gives to us when we are quiet before Him. That's the time when we can dare to let things come to the surface. It's a bit like taking the bandages off and discovering the state of the injuries. Maybe the value of the initial praise element in our services is that it can start to disarm us of our fears about God and establishes His interest in us. It can penetrate that feeling of separation we've perhaps allowed to happen. This isn't always so, especially if the music drives you further away. So, Worship Leader, you have a great responsibility as God's nursing assistant!

We need to let God Write The Songs, metaphorically and perhaps literally, by being discerning in our musical aims. We need to allow Him to Write The Songs in our worship by giving space for Him to be there, and to speak to us. The way in which we regard God will have a trickle down effect, and should affect how we regard others, and the needs of our common worship life. Although that can be a case of "one man's ceiling is another man's floor", we all should be accommodated in our worship needs.

I want you to imagine that the following is a message from God:-

"Do you know how long I've been alive? Always! Do you know who had the idea for the first song ever? Me! I created all those black and white dancing notes that would hang together perfectly, like the thread of a fabulous string of pearls. I just knew that I could use them to write my messages of love across your heart, and everything else that's special in life. I knew they would help you to sing, and cry, and love. Do you know that I designed you with a place where only I can go? I've hidden it right inside you - a deep, sparkling lake where you and I can be together, a place that makes us both feel young, even Ancient Me! It's where that secret life inside us can feel free to jump out to dance! I made my music in such a way as to let you all celebrate in a different way.

Most of all, I made it to fill the holes in your heart because you're special, and I love you."

Did you enjoy that? Did it go "wow" in your soul? I hope so! You probably haven't realised that you have just read the sentiments of a song, written by Bruce Johnston, and sung by that ultimate King of Schmaltz, the one and only Barry Manilow, that silver voiced seducer of (mainly!) female hearts everywhere! I hope that any "blokey blokes" reading this will not feel threatened by the B.M. association! What Bruce did manage to achieve was to express his conviction about God being the Source of a joyous gift - the "Finger of God" creation that "oils the wheels that make our world go round". He wanted to express the spirit of creativity that resides within each of us. It's where God has left "a chair", so that He can sit down and spend time with us. Music, that gift from God's heart, lights our world with a great luminosity, inspiring, reviving and healing us in our sorrows, as well as stirring and tenderising us. We need, therefore, to safeguard it and not exploit unnecessarily, or use it unwisely, It is, of course, subject to individual integrity as to what is deemed appropriate! Christians are urged to "make a joyful noise unto the Lord", so let's do joyful - but not hideous! There's a prayer by Jeff Lucas that encapsulates these sentiments: "Father God, when my mindset is being shaped by my culture more than by You, renew my mind again by Your Spirit. Amen". The most important thing to remember is that "Worship is the one thing God cannot do to Himself. In order to worship, you have to worship something higher than yourself".

I'd like to end with a request. In the midst of our twenty first century concept of Church and particularly its worship life, can we somehow guard against the more superficial elements that can so easily turn it into Big Top entertainment? Can we try to find commonality that makes for Rowland's Hut unity? After all, who Writes The Songs? ? God Writes The Songs!

Chapter 8: Carol Says

"Whatever He Says To You, Do It." "The Witness"
- Jimmy and Carol Owens
- John 2 v.5

We all have at least one person in our lives whom we tend to make the point of reference for matters both great and small. There have been several in my life, their words and phrases indelibly branded into my word bank and becoming household terms of reference that fit a particular bill. Many has been the occasion when my husband and I have quoted the appropriate saying at exactly the same time, usually incomprehensible to the outside world, but making perfect sense to us. It illustrates how adept we are at living in a world of code where our conversational "dots and dashes" can be translated by our inner handbook of interpretation. Like "The Sound of Music", I've chosen just a few of my favourite things to appear here. They belong to extraordinary people who, in this setting, have brought me food for literary thought, as well as help in my hour of need.

It was only when I was in conversation with some close friends that I started listening to myself, and discovering just how frequently my sentences began with my now legendary "Carol Says"! I can almost hear you saying, "Who's she?" I first came across Carol at a church we started to attend in our current home town. Music and singing being our "thing", my guitarist husband and my singing self were soon grafted into the worship scene (an area that should always be handled with integrity and sensitivity). There were numerous talented musicians and singers among the ranks, some of whom were in the process of making a professionally produced worship album. Carol was was one of them, a songbird of both Christian worship and outside jazz gigs, and equally comfortable in either. Singing is her life force, her raison d'être, the inner self-regulating metronome of her normality. Painting is also a channel for her creativity, but I don't think it's as crucial to her well-being as her need to sing. The musicians proved to be an adaptable bunch, mixing and matching with comparative ease. I often found myself paired with Carol, sharing and enjoying the melodic and harmonic lines of the beautiful Vineyard songs that had become the musical diet. She's a "heart on sleeve" kinda girl, wearing her emotions, particularly crying, like a favourite jumper!

She didn't come across me - at least, not in the personal sense, until much later. These days, we meet on a fairly ad hoc basis, and usually in today's sophisticated equivalent of the coffee bars of our "Rock around the clock" youth, both of us now a bit more "clock" than "rock"! There's no conversational stone left unturned, the topics ranging from dogs to destiny, hairstyles to Heaven, fashion to faith! My description of Carol's role in life is that she sits up in "the watchtower", surveying the land in a spiritual sense, much like the prophets of old. She keeps an eye on the comings and goings of the world, both sacred and secular, and isn't afraid to voice her opinions on the signs of the times. The confident manner in which she delivers these opinions can't fail to engage your attention, consequently forming an arguably orderly queue in your mind. At any given conversational moment, and like an inflatable bouncy castle, complete with flag, up they triumphantly and assertively pop!

Because Carol has a "skin-on-skin" relationship with God, it pays to consider her spiritual insights. She's a child of the living God who, like all of us was rescued from the decisions of a previous bitter-sweet pathway that had left its mark and had caused pain - a life she's not afraid to own up to. She cries, laughs and loves in equal measure, possessing an immediate empathy that she's not afraid to give away. When the chips have been down in my life, it's Carol who's been the open door to Rowland's Hut. She's the one who takes you by the hand leads you back into believing you are God's valuable Daughter. However, I have come to realise that some of the ideas she shares and the positions she holds are as a result of the place she's reached on her path of faith. They are not automatically transferable to others. We need to ask ourselves whether opinion, advice or position is necessarily wise and applicable to our own lives. That said, it's always stimulating to be shaken and stirred by Carol, her appetite and enthusiasm spilling over like choice champagne, a welcome positive in a negative world. I'm grateful to know that, like Sir Thomas More, there's a "Carol Says" for all seasons!

"All the King's horses and all the King's men, couldn't put Humpty together again".
(A nursery rhyme - traditional).

Much like the bacon, Marietta came to Britain from Denmark. As with the famous Danish loaf, she was soft to the touch yet totally resilient. At the time of our friendship, she was busy teaching her young son to speak and read Danish so that he could communicate with his maternal extended family - at least, that's what I thought. Marietta was also a friend of God, worshipping at our church and also a friend of many. She was putting herself through the academic graduate route, financing her course by working in her husband's family's slot machine emporium. She sat in a little money changing booth, (reminiscent of biblical times!), depositing change to the pleasure seekers of the seaside town, a few stones throws down the coast from our more genteel haven. It was during one of our coffee conversations that Marietta launched into a description of her work scene, at the same time instructing her son from a Danish cookbook! I don't know if it was because of her restricted view in the booth, or whether it was down to her quaint Scandinavian expressions, but her description of the humanity that had passed in front of her eyes was one of "pieces of people". In an instant, I knew just what she saw and meant! It suggested a tutti frutti, fruit salad selection of body parts, a disturbing image reminiscent of scary medieval paintings! It was a watershed moment, when a coffee and a Danish took on a whole new meaning!

Like a puff of wind dispersing a dandelion clock, Marietta disappeared from our lives. With the utmost secrecy (and with hindsight, the maximum of long term planning), she and her son, minus husband, had relocated to Denmark. It all began to add up - the academic preparation for her future economic survival, the Danish lessons, the job that required her to sit on her "pieces of people" perch.....

Her Houdini-like exit took some getting used to. There were to be no more coffees in the sunny cafe, no more cheerful chats with the blue eyed blonde who was alternative in fashion and phrases, and no more faith-sharing in That Hut! I really don't know why the words of "Log Cabin Home In The Sky" have come to mind at this point. Maybe it's something to do with Danish forests and secluded dwelling places in the peace and quiet of the countryside. Maybe Marietta felt the need to hide or to get away for a while, "to a place where a man can be free as the wind" (sorry, girls!). Maybe she, like the Country and Western song, felt that "winter is nigh, let us fly to that log cabin home in the sky". Whatever the reasons that propelled her from our shores, I hope she recovered some happiness in her native homeland and managed to find a Rowland's Hut of comfort and familiarity.

There seemed to be a stunned silence between all the people who had held Marietta in common, a rather reverent but conspiratorial silence. It transpired that just one person had been trusted and sworn to secrecy with The Plan - and kept it that way! It wasn't long before Marietta's son started to visit his dad during school holidays - but never with his mum.

Very sadly, Marietta is no longer here - or indeed, there. Her death was reputed to be the result of a brain haemorrhage, denying the world of our blue denimed, people-watching, quaintly worded Marietta. One day, we'll meet again, where the pieces will make a whole. Au revoir, Marietta!

"It's Only Wirdz" (with deepest apologies to The Bee Gees).

Right from the time of Mr. Tucker, that superb English teaching mentor of my junior school days, I have harboured a lifelong passion for words. My teacher was rigorous, instructing us to look up all meanings and their application, and sending us home with "challenges". Consequently, words now magnetise, seduce and inspire me. It's fascinating to see how language is used and adapted, the latter being sometimes irritating, depending on how purist you want to be! One of my current pet hates is the rapidly spreading use of "haitch" instead of "aitch" - as in "haitch P sauce"! I vividly remember our junior school teachers fearlessly stamping out that particular mispronunciation. Another one is when someone is asked how they are and the person replies, "Good, thanks" .....! No one was asking about behaviour! As for the way in which the word "awesome" is abused, I'm rendered speechless. I'm fairly sure God must be too!

I feel that the next person deserves the "Sergeant Pepper" treatment, so, "May I introduce to you, the one and only" - no, not Billy Shears, but Nikki! Making an entrance to our lives thirty two years and two hundred days ago. (thought you'd like a bit of precision!), she has proved to be a tireless source of drive and energy, putting her shoulder (and possibly other body parts) to any passing wheel of life. She entered and exited our new home at some speed, en route to her beloved Boys Brigade, which she ruled with the proverbial rod of iron. She was highly successful in that supercharged atmosphere of Boys' World, endearing herself, and her welcome structure and discipline, to boys large, small and decidedly stroppy! She took on the challenge with gusto, relish and probably enough sauce to smother - but in reality, to mother the cartload of monkeys in her charge! Her many outings were legendary, often seen commanding the troops as they headed for one of the local beaches, where they could let rip. The pleasure would have been totally mutual! Nikki is still approached in the street by grown men who were once Brigade lads, and who wish to be remembered as such. What a testament to this dedicated lady!

Nikki has had many practical outlets for expressing her life and her Christian faith. Not exactly a house group kind of girl, she was heard to say, "I'd go if I could take the ironing board with me under my arm".....! This seems the appropriate place in which to mention her unique ability with words. I need to give just a couple of choice examples to illustrate her gift. On talking about a book she was reading, she told me that the author wrote under a persuado - a far more expressive description than the rather dark and more mysterious pseudonym. It certainly persuaded me! The second and equally impressive re-naming concerned the subject of cooking. On comparing our new ovens and their performances, Nikki, with the utmost gravity, announced that her oven was a psychotherm...... Hmmm, couldn't agree more. I'd often wondered just what, or maybe whom I was grappling with in my kitchen - obviously a much more menacing enemy than the circotherms of saner ovens!

Well known for being the outings planner, Nikki was never happier than walking and looking after other people's dogs, hiking along canals in the pouring rain or acting like the Pied Piper in taking assorted children out in prams, on trams or on foot to a favourite Italian ice cream emporium (and taking some home for the freezer - the ice cream, probably not the children!). Visits to craft mills, coach outings (a particularly famous one where Nikki nearly ended up driving the coach through narrow Welsh lanes) and Kentucky Fried lunches or teas have all been done to perfection. There was the legendary trip to Windermere, where we ladies went happily home with our handbags full of Cumberland sausages! Our almost world - famous "Tiara Club" drew together those females with a predilection for fairy wings and - yes, you've guessed it, the wearing of tiaras! There was one particular summer's evening when Nikki ran (maybe even flew) down the street, resplendent in both.....! The Club was really an excuse for female bonding and the consumption of delicious meals, sometimes of the takeaway variety and firmly served by someone whose tiara - and serving spoon, demanded supreme authority and submission from we lesser mortals. Two of our lovely girls are sadly no longer with us, but I hope they're now wearing their eternal tiaras - and maybe wings? Chris and Julie, we salute you (with our wands), and we'll definitely be able to recognise you!

If there are sandwiches to be made, cakes to be baked and mountains of washing up to be done for parties, celebrations or funerals, Nikki's your girl - the doyenne of the sink! She's a number cruncher, list maker, chair arranger and quiche cutter. She doesn't suffer fools, gladly or otherwise, and Her Methods Rule! Most events at the church bear her unmistakable hallmarks, and most wouldn't stand much chance without her underpinning. She and her husband have recently embarked upon a new venture. The ARK, the acronym for Alive, Retired and Kicking, provides a programme of activities and stimulation for older people. A valuable and welcome asset, it encompasses topics such as art, horticulture, bowls, genealogy, musical entertainment, "you name it and they'll do it", and most crucially, food! The three day events (for people, not horses!) give everyone attending an experience to remember. I applaud Nikki's vision for reaching out to the community with her interpretation of the message of God's love. Craft mornings are also firmly under her organisational wing, drawing many from the local community outside the Church. As well as producing handmade goods, they share outings, celebratory meals and an annual holiday together, all perfectly organised by the smoother of the inevitable ruffled feathers! Fridays have seen their share of dramas, including the odd ambulance having to be called to poorly ladies, Nikki handling such upsets with her usual calm and common sense.

The celebratory tables were turned, so to speak, on the occasion of her sixtieth birthday. Her daughter, with the utmost military precision, had planned a surprise party that she would host in her own home. In order to preserve the secret, Nikki was led to believe that she was meeting her family at a local restaurant. With deceit of the highest level!, I spent many beguiling conversations with Nikki, reassuring her over her uncertainties as to whether she and her husband would need jackets for going home in the late evening, and how she should dress in general for the fictitious, but, by now, strangely believable restaurant scenario. My totally convincing performance should still make me worried! All went to plan and Nikki was led into the room where the surprise guests, having arrived from all points of the globe, was holding its collective breath. Nikki's face was the proverbial picture! It took a while for her to comprehend the scene in front of her, working her way round the assembled guests in a daze. However, it all resulted in being a huge success. She received a sparkling array of pretty and practical presents, beautiful blooms of both plants and cut flowers, and of course, fabulous food and drink. As if planned, it was a hot and sunny summer's evening, the guests being able to spill out through the conservatory and into the garden. As they say, a good time was had by all, especially The Party Girl! Ten action packed years later, Nikki planned her own seventieth birthday celebration, this time to be held in the church hall, and in the form of an Abba evening. I wasn't able to attend this splendid event, but on being urged to "come and Abba good time", they all surely did! I eagerly await (and somewhat prematurely anticipate) the theme of her eightieth!

So, that's Nikki, a funny, down-the-middle, no-nonsense, "port in THE storm" (not any old port in a storm!) "salt of the earth" kind of girl, a "card for everyone's birthday" kind of girl a visitor of the sick, and a shoulder to cry on kind of girl. She's the person you would go to in a crisis, the person with common sense, the person who invites you into Rowland's Hut. Together, with Carol and Marietta, may she shine, and may their words twinkle like stars in your sky! By the way, have you heard the one about the "Morning Dance Of The Seven Vests", performed each day by Nikki's husband? Has anyone told you about Nikki's walk with the dog, the duck, the goose and the frog? Thought not!

Extras.

Like walk. - on actors in a play, there have been times in my life when words have played more of a cameo role. They have been passing phases, (or should that be phrases?) but nevertheless still significant, and cemented firmly into my being, ready to pop up from the dark recesses of my memory. One such trigger is that of parent and child, the recollections of my children's verbal cuteness guaranteed to light the smouldering wick of intolerance - and worse! Only recently, I was given the withering look and speech of remonstration of "it was thirty years ago, Mum", fame! I have to admit that when I was in the hot seat of my own parental reminiscences, it also curled my brain and toes to be subjected to the humiliation of regurgitated child-speak! Since the death of my parents, I have come to realise that our oral traditions are vital. We need to pass on our memories, the giving of them creating a fabric of existence and marking a place in family history. There's a visceral need deep within our very cells to acquire the knowledge of the formation of our childhood characters. To me, it now seems as essential as our fingerprints, a verbal proof of existence on our journey to maturity, and proof that someone cared enough to carry such knowledge in the Rowland's Hut of his or her heart.

When one of my sons was small, he used to to talk about banging his "arm-bows" - a brilliantly succinct description of those knobbly bits! His take on the name for raw fish was "sea-shoe", a much more romantic offering than the conventional "sushi". His understanding of a song at church that talked of God being exalted was that "The God of our salvation be exhausted"..... I'm sure that He must have been, considering that He had all of us to look after! In passing through her own "phase of phrase", my eldest grand-daughter made her linguistic mark by her oft repeated statement of "Don't be so memanding, mummy" - a compact combination of demanding and moaning!

I happen to live in a place where there are still lots of individual shops, the owners possessing a rich seam of personalities, and providing a much more personal service than the standard chains of shops our towns now normally allow. I value their words and expressions, adding both warmth humour, and shape to my day. Over the time I've lived there, the owners have come and gone but a few have been a constant presence. One of my favourite characters is a twinkly man with just a hint of naughtiness about his weathered person, a man who's lived a bit and loved a lot. During his working day, a notice periodically appears on his shop window, advising you that "he's gone for ten, back later". My mind doesn't boggle any more about the nature of "ten", as the tens have run into thousands, if not millions! His other favourite window message is "If you don't see what you want in the window, please ask inside". On mentioning that I hadn't yet seen him in the window, he was genuinely taken aback, and at the same time, somewhat flattered!

No reflection about people is complete without including That Time Of Year that makes grown men cry, head for the hills or the pub, and urges women to join the ritual stampede to the shops, and encase themselves in sellotape! With this in mind, what is to follow is the result of one of those serendipitous events in life. I recently happened to be clearing out a top shelf of a cupboard, when I came across a carefully wrapped object. It proved to be the Christmas book I'd created some years ago, a compilation of impressions recorded in their own handwriting, by family and friends of a particular Christmas. Here were those comments - and the people, jumping off the pages to make a fascinating read! They were faithful reflections of each person's character, making me feel that they were actually talking to me! This "pieces of people" compendium was too significant to miss, so having thrilled and filled my heart, I'll let it enter yours.

"A Slice Of Christmas".

"When like stars His children crowned, All in white shall wait around".

Ann: "Snowy, frosty Christmas, bright Boxing Day, amazing night skies, clear bright moons and fantastic shades of changing blacks to blues, towards daylight".

Daniel: "First Christmas with Kath".

Kathryn: "First Christmas back home. Wonderful!".

Jane: "Bill's footprints in the snow, and then Bill trying to catch a snowflake and eat it!". (Bill's the cat!)".

Matt: "Wish I'd saved the After Eights till Christmas".

Sadie: "how lovely and unique the average person is. Here's to each and every person encountered this year".

Jamie: (He was true to form - had signed his name but hadn't written his comment. Probably said "I'll fill it in later" but never did. In his defence, he was in the hospitality trade, so was always working at festive times!).

Ann: "forgot the cheese biscuits. Left them in the shop, so someone got lucky! Serving Christmas dinner doesn't get any easier! Made trifles at 6 am in the dark black sky that turned to blue". Lovely to see everyone sitting round the Boxing Day table on Keith's birthday, the girls all glam, the boys handsome! Attended some beautiful and moving Christmas music and services, lovely presents from my family and friends. Dan, Kath and Ollie's charity recital was wonderful".

Keith: "lovely to celebrate my (Boxing Day) birthday with everyone round our table. Great to have Kath here with Daniel for her first Christmas with us. Unfortunately, it was the first year my mother couldn't be here".

Bill (the cat) : "The smell of roast turkey has driven me mad!".

Richard: "Plenty of drink and ducks for Xmas. What a performance of The Messiah! ".

Rosemary: "Chaos all around but we've been lucky. Good food and music".

David: "Counting my blessings, a better year than last, last year went quite slowly, this year's gone too fast. When I was young, Christmas came so slowly and went so quickly, gone! Now everything about Christmas seems like formula!".

Nikki: "How time has flown! Where is my tiara? Where is anything? Where am I? The snow was great but cold and wet. David had a mandolin for Christmas! He'll be wearing it soon!".

John: "What is it all about. I wish someone would let me know! Still, I have much to be grateful for - compared to many others in the world!".
P.S. "When will Emma get sorted out?".

Wendy: "A lovely Christmas Day after all the stress and rushing around. The snow was a bonus and made it magical. Can't believe it's all over for another year!".

Chris: "This year was quiet! In some ways I didn't like it! No boys around. But the rest was needed. Never imagined it would be like this! Feet up, telly on, chocs and chilling out. Lovely!".

Pauline: "This Christmas I felt so blessed to have both daughters, son in laws and five grandchildren on Xmas Day and the children slept over and all ran in our bedroom to greet us on Boxing Day".

Phil: "This Christmas is, as usual, a time for the family. We were very pleased and blessed at having them all together".

Godfrey: "The joys of comings and goings of all our family to share this very special time in the Church's year".

Carol: "One day to celebrate such a wonderful birth. Surely we need more days of slobbing out and getting drunk! May love abound this new year".

Nigel: "There is an inevitability about Christmas. It is like a thunderstorm from which there is no escape!".

David D: "I enjoyed this Christmas. I was in Arneside and it was very peaceful. Wasn't the White Christmas great?".

Janet: "I had a very relaxing Christmas at Georgie's, with snow on Christmas Day - very beautiful. Then on to Edinburgh over New Year. I was spoiled absolutely rotten with far too many presents. On New Years Eve we went to a service at St. Cuthberts. We came out at 11.55 just in time for the fireworks - the earth shook!! We had a great view."

Christine: "What made Christmas special for me was spending it with my family. Lots of time to enjoy being with each other always makes it special!! I'm looking forward to another good year!"

David J: "This Christmas had it all - busy family times with children arriving and departing - and quiet times to think about the BIRTH that gives our lives meaning and provides for our eternal destiny".

It's several years since we all made those significant jottings. I expect you may want to hear how John now has the answer to his dilemma over Emma. She's just finishing a degree and is getting married any time soon! Wendy balances normal living, and the various combinations of pills, alongside many medical appointments. David now wears two handmade mandolins and ten bass guitars (not handmade), and Nikki feels like wrapping them, scarf-like, round his instrumentally shaped neck! Sadie, my mum, passed peacefully away, after what seemed like a world heavyweight fight for stubbornly held independence. Keith's mum also passed peacefully away after complete support, at the grand old age of nearly ninety seven. Chris, my best Tiara friend (another page, another chapter), also suddenly, prematurely, and tragically passed away, leaving a gaping wide hole amongst the Tiara Girls. Bill the cat has been dethroned by the arrival of two brilliant little boys, and Daniel and Kath have been blessed with two equally brilliant little girls, (my grandchildren, so totally biased!). Richard passed away, taking with him a massive zest for life. Godfrey retired from being a cheerful, solid, larger than life, horse riding vicar, and Phil and Pauline sold their holiday home, no longer adding their Christian warmth and faithfulness to our area. Carol continues to be Carol, as only she can be, and Nigel still maintains his tentative and exasperated relationship with the world, particularly the Christian one! David J. tries to cope without Chris, his soul-mate and anchor, continuing to be blown around by the winds of loneliness and lack of purpose, whilst David D. has relocated to his beloved Arnside, but is still happily roving around on trains, sometimes bumping into him, en passant, at our main station. Keith, my husband, has also acquired a handmade mandolin, but so far hasn't been driven to wear it as an extra winter layer! I have crocheted and written my way into the Guinness Book a Of Records (in my dreams!), having swathed the whole world in treble stitched throws and very many words. Janet has had a hobbling time of it, having undergone surgery on her foot, and Christine receives a lot of support to keep her life as safe as possible, her daughter, son in law and grandchildren still being integral to her life, and on hand when necessary.

My "Slice Of Christmas" ended with a memory page, a dedication to those Mums and Dads, Grandmas and Grandads, Aunties and Uncles, friends, colleagues and acquaintances who now stand "On Another Shore", but whose footprints are indelible across the memory path of my life. Since that written crystallisation of people and events, several family's branches have budded, including ours. My husband and I now have the privilege of our most beautiful grandchildren, the next generation, who have brought much joy and meaning to our lives. With this in mind, I am resolute that they should also record their Christmas thoughts, so my very next seasonal aim is to produce "Another Slice Of Christmas"! So, Friends, Romans, any passing Greeks bearing gifts and the inevitable Countrymen, lend me your ears. I'll be at your door, pen in hand!

To have a phrase or saying spring to mind at an appropriate moment is often a source of humour and joy, a resonating kind of shorthand or code, making total sense of a situation and carrying a bigger meaning and application to other areas in our lives. A friend of mine has an almost mantra- like pronouncement, that "God moves in mysterious ways". He certainly does, and seemingly covering all bases, from the Lottery to the provision of doughnuts at her church coffee break - or rather, the sudden removal of that stickily comforting crutch, the previous passport to an otherwise alien human landscape! Joking aside, He moves in this framework more than we give Him credit for, because He loves us and knows "our feeble frame" and often hanging by equally feeble threads in our faith life. I'm glad He's more merciful to us than we are to Him, and our fellow men. My once razor sharp mind, (now a more soft focus haze!), has just remembered that Jesus is described as "The Word". How wonderful is that? It means that He can write on us, and we can "read" Him and "speak" Him. We can glimpse beyond the edge of our finite, feet of clay state to a future far more glorious than we can comprehend right now!

Chapter 9: It's A Load Of Old Conkerers!

"We are more than Conquerors through Him that loved us."
- Romans 8. V 37

This has all the makings of a small, but perfectly formed rant, so I suggest you concentrate on the "perfectly formed" bit! The title of this polemic is based on a friend's complaints, made many moons ago at our mid week Christian meetings. There were aspects of teaching not to his exact delight, as they didn't feel right, and more to the point, he felt they were rubbish! Consequently, "It's a load of old conkers" became his verbal outlet for his frustrations! At this point, I would like to publicly thank him for bequeathing this useful, succinct and coded shorthand! It's one of those "must have" phrases for examining life's frustrations, and I admit to having mentally applied it on numerous occasions, and to various speakers and situations. It's been a useful yardstick by which to measure either throwaway statements, or those opinions that are often tucked away, almost subliminally, in talks, messages or sermons (according to your ecclesiastical terms of reference!). They appear as glittering little gems, but upon closer investigation, are nothing more than imitations - maybe convincing imitations, but nevertheless, not the real thing. This is often the case when we actually bother to weigh things against Scripture, allowing, of course, for legitimate interpretational differences.

The burning question is, how do we distinguish between what seems genuine in our spiritual quest, and what is fake? Are things the product of the Zeitgeist - the spirit and fashion of the age, and the almost giddy desire for the passing trends of "now"? Are they a beguiling and deceptive red herring, with a quick fix label? Is our personal integrity and discernment developed and alert enough to distinguish between truth and lie? Are others willing to listen to our viewpoint, and more importantly, is it ever received, or are we sidelined as not being of the correct spiritual calibre? Do others recognise our God given insights and ability to reflect wisdom and guidance? Are others willing to validate our humanity and spirituality? Do they allow us to contribute to the corporate direction of the Church? Or are we conditioned by the white coated figures of authority in our spiritual guidance, only listening to pastors, preachers and those who shout the loudest in their proclamations of God's intentions, instead of the Still, Small Voice? These are big questions, deserving of a proper exploration of who we are, how we see ourselves, and how we are seen and regarded by others. We need to think about our relational and spiritual roles, and the place they hold in our daily lives, our Church, and our fellowship circles.

What exactly do I mean by the "Conkerers" of the title? Like the horse chestnut that's prepared for battle by being soaked in vinegar, rendered hard and shiny, and then dangled from a string, we can become regrettably similar. We dangle from the string of "self" threaded through our middles, ready to do combat with any other hard and shiny individual willing to take us on in a fight. There are some people who are like the conker that has just fallen off the tree. They lie on the floor, encased in their outer spiky shell, and not yet hardened, either deliberately or through the consequences of life. At this stage, there's still hope that, like the conker, the individual hiding inside the protective shell can be coaxed out, softened, helped to stand befriended. We've been designed in such a way as to need others, to befriend others, and to work together with others. This is especially so in the way the Church is meant to function, including the importance of hearing God's plans and intentions, and interpreting them for the greater good. In order to be the kind of conqueror that God wants us to be, we have to resist the temptation to be a "Conkerer", (word, mine), someone who, in the spirit of a folk song, "Goes A Conkerin", knocking against others to fend them off, and with the intention of "getting one over" on them. God wants us to be overcomers in the sense of not being combative, of finding unity and strength in each other, and in learning to submit to each other. We've actually been promised that we will be "more than conquerors" - more than being pickled in vinegar, threaded with string and used as a weapon of war!

You would think that the Church would be the one place where we can find our identity and a sense of belonging, an opportunity to leave behind the loneliness and alienation of the world, and a society in which to feel safe and wanted - a Rowland's Hut that is as close to God's Heavenly model as is possible on earth. However, the current styles of Church organisation, particularly the large gatherings based on the Mega and Community Church models, are not conducive to close relational and meaningful ties. The members tend to be drawn from distances far outside the area, making it less likely for there to be a day to day local network. Additionally, they are less likely to be able to rely on midweek small groups, that give much needed support and significance, and provides an anchor to the unwieldy larger Sunday gathering. The recent adoption in society of the idea of "The Hub", computer language for the port, or place of interconnection has also been translated into Church concept terms. The central gathering is the place from which power is drawn, acting as a reference point, to inform and sustain the various group activities, or hubs that are planted in the community and beyond.

These models of Church are more likely to focus on big programmes of service in the community, leaders being prone to quoting percentages of those members who are engaged in "serving", as their measure of good spiritual health. This is linked with the idea that you begin to "fly" as a sign of personal success. Maybe it's good imagery, but then there's the thought that you have to learn how to fall first, before you soar upwards with your wings......? When the frustration of the pressure of this rises in me, I'm driven to thinking that maybe they should put up one of those thermometer - type boards, displaying their money raising targets and achievements towards a new roof, spire,or organ, the sort that we don't really see any more. In this instance, the board would be flushed with pride at just how successful the campaign to "serve" has been! On a serious level, it is indeed a good, and Godly aim to want to serve God in whatever capacity we're drawn to. It allows us to grow, develops our latent skills, and inspires us, both practically and spiritually in pointing others to God. However, we must beware of thinking that everyone who's engaged in acts of service is automatically "tickety boo", and "connected" to the Body of Believers. In asserting that Christians are designed to serve God in some capacity, we mustn't assume that those around us are running along quite happily, like so many wound up clockwork toys. A person's fragile emotional state is often disguised or worse, hidden, by seeming activity. It's important to bear in mind that well worn but useful saying - that we're human beings, not human doings!

I'm finding that the leadership style of such Churches is often underpinned with strongly held agendas, and single minded and deceptively rigid pathways. This usually means that its leaders tend not to listen to anything outside their own heads, and are dismissive of input from "the shop floor" that might be ultimately for the greater good. In trying to discuss a genuine area of difficulty, my personal experience resulted in my being told that it might be better to go elsewhere - definitely not the type of Christian leadership that considered me important enough to be listened to! Talk about falling on deaf ears! I believe it was actually Jesus who said, "He that has ears to hear, LET HIM HEAR"! We have to be careful not to become dulled in our hearing, and preconditioned in our thinking. It's not that we should demand others to do exactly what we think and say, this being clearly wrong. It's more about listening to each other and looking to God for guiding principles and better choices, rather than short term satisfactions and what can be an insidious self-rule. It's about acknowledging that as Christian believers, we all have a contribution and a part to play in the governance of our corporate lives, After all, isn't this the Body Ministry talked about and demonstrated in the Early Church, an example we are exhorted to follow and by which great store is set?

I expect that there are a number of today's Believers who are either unaware, or choose not to model themselves upon the precepts of our Early Church Fathers, seeing themselves as too urbane, too sophisticated or too individualistic to allow themselves to consider the input of others. If we're not careful, Church can just become a pit stop for self expression and sensual gratification. It's encouraged by a prevailing and pervading attitude of giving the people what they want, in order to both attract and keep them in a church building, particularly so in the area of music worship. It's widely assumed that if they are not provided with the same level of noise and style as the world outside, they won't come to meet with God. I regard that as being the lowest common denominator for evaluating the spiritual needs, sensitivities, and resulting provisions for congregations. We also need to consider the needs of different age groups in the corporate arena, as being prepared to ride roughshod over legitimate concerns over style and content is tantamount to children having a conker fight. We then become "Conkerers", as opposed to "Conquerors". When we enter Church life, it is on a voluntary basis, humanly speaking. We are willing (hopefully!) in our spiritual quest, to submit ourselves to the teaching and leading of others. We don't expect to be emotionally and spiritually "mugged" and dictated to, but to share the common life as believers in Jesus Christ.

A recent tragedy in our Church has highlighted the problem that we don't always know what's going on under the surface of people's lives. I appreciate that we can't second guess the intentions of those around us, and that we're not responsible for someone's course of action. I'm hoping, however, that we, as a Church, will regard what happened as a serious wake up call and a warning not to take people for granted. Christians aren't perfect people, and don't have the monopoly in promoting emotionally healthy living, but we do worship a God who comes to the aid of all people, and who is always available to help them. I'm not convinced that, given the frenetic drive to move forwards, onwards, and upwards (that surely being everyone's aim!), it will remain a conscious and long term concern to look below the surface in the human evaluation process, such is the pace of activity, and the way in which things move on. I'm hoping to be proved wrong, and that in its efforts to fulfil the mandate of what I label as "service evangelism" for the world outside, there will also be times of oasis for the gathered church, allowing its collective soul to be fed and watered, its wrinkles smoothed, and its spirit refreshed.

We need to get beyond the superficial levels of the average Church gathering, where communication is often limited to the action of a snooker table, where the various balls fly round and end up in the right pockets, with the assumption that all must be well. We need to be on the lookout for balls that aren't in the right pockets, any pockets, or that have disappeared from view, maybe having rolled off, only to be found under the table. If we're to go out there and "love our neighbour as ourselves", then firstly, we have to be able to love ourselves. The responsibility of the leaders is to make sure that they are serving enough "food" for the inner person, nutrition that is worthy of God's children. We can't just exist on a spiritual fast food diet, the "E" numbers only equipping us for speed, noise and endless action - "a load of old conkers" presumption if ever there was one!

God doesn't use a key to wind us up, like those clockwork toys of our childhoods (some of our childhoods, anyway!), and leaving us to lurch along until we run out of steam - we can do that all by ourselves! To make God's love, approval, and purposes appear conditional, and dependent upon our "doing", is yet another of those "load of old conkers" misconceptions! God doesn't dangle that recent nauseous and overworked governmental phrase, "hard working people" over us, to produce a feeling of shame, and as a prerequisite for receiving what are essential entitlements. He doesn't goad us to conform and submit in that patronising "carrot and stick" manner. God doesn't love us because of our "output", but wants us to receive His "input" because of His love for us. By nature, we're more attuned to the Mary and Martha scenario, where we would prefer to "work our way", rather than receive something for nothing, contrary to that insidious governmental manipulative attitude. As humans, I don't believe we're comfortable at sitting still and receiving, often feeling that we don't deserve it, and have to earn it - another "conkers" moment!

Then there's Society's demands to be a "someone", a "celebrity", with some of us having to project our individuality to the point of always finding ways of drawing attention to ourselves. Regrettably, this need that has jumped straight from the world-view, hasn't left the Church untouched, encroaching on situations it really shouldn't, and encouraging unhealthy personality cults. There are those of us who see ourselves as "independent", perhaps having always been taught that we have to "go it alone", that it's down to ourselves to stand or fall, succeed or fail. We retreat behind our castle walls, either out of pride that we know best, or out of fear that we don't know what we're doing, but can't let anyone see, or let anyone in to help. Again, we're in "conkers" territory.

If I were to subtitle this section, I would call it, "I'd like to help but I'm a Christian"! Now, on the surface, this sounds facetious and cynical. It's like one of those brickbats thrown by atheists and critics at those struggling to follow Christ through all the complexities and failures of life, so what could I possibly mean by it? A recent conversation with a very sick friend revealed that, as a Christian, and humanly speaking, she felt she was all on her own. Apart from her many medical appointments, she's restricted to her own four walls. No one visits her from the church she used to attend - a church with the label " Community" attached to it. In withdrawing the doughnuts they used to serve with the coffee after their services (much to my friend's disappointment, as they provided a bit of comfort!), they also, on the surface, appear to have withdrawn their care - either in, or out, of the said Community. I personally don't think this is the entire picture, but I do think it illustrates just how careless and casual we can all be in our awareness, accountability, and organisational strategies.

It begs the question as to whether we are practising a vested interest form of Christianity, where the emphasis is on putting our own needs first, and finding effective ways of getting them met. This could be through gaining social status by attaching ourselves to a church with a reputation for doing a lot in the community, and whose members tend to blow their own trumpet. Some of us gain attention by always having enough problems to talk about, without wanting them solved. Others use church as a drug on which to get "high", either through wild worship or extreme spiritual activity. We need to seek God in the deeper places, but we should make sure we drink from the right wells of water, as not all of them are going to be sweet and fresh. Settling for these diversions can restrict our spirituality to "Me-ness". We can be tempted to display the same behaviour as the Corinthian Church members, whose prevalent cultural attitudes led them to think that their faith life was about a game of one-upmanship, wanting to be seen as more "spiritual" than their neighbours, We most certainly do follow "too much the devices and desires of our own hearts"! This can result in a "chest of drawers and filing system" mentality, deliberately, or inadvertently being careless and selective in our relationships, and avoiding commitments to others. Like an assortment of folded clothes, we put people into certain mental "drawers", the labelling of which encompasses the following:

Not now.
Not ever.
Can't be bothered.
Sometime in the future.
Haven't time now. I'll do it for you later. (They don't.)
Do I have to?
I'm sorry. I'm too busy.
I can't talk to you now. I want to worship.
It's too hard.
Not me!
I forgot.
I need to go and speak to someone (more important, that is).
I'll phone, text, arrange to meet. (They don't) .
I'm too shy.
I'm too inadequate.
We'll have to vet you before you can.......be in the worship group because firstly, you have to be a worshipper(?)........serve communion,......pray out loud, ...preach, etc. We'll get back to you. (They don't.)

(Please feel free to add your own!).

None of this is encouraging to those seeking God and relationships within the Church, a Rowland's Hut amongst God's people, and searching for a new kind of acceptance and significance. Despite the fact we're all flawed, and that some of the reasons on the above list might at times be legitimate, our aim and example should be to model and experience a new society, one that sees all people as equally deserving, and where they can have their broken spirits mended. Otherwise, we're liable to indulge in self-love, rather than love of each other, producing a misuse of personal power and leadership. We need also to guard against male "rule" (and rules!), with its "divide and conquer" tendencies. It's like the worship song says, we're to prefer the needs of others. We have to realise that the hallmarks of God's character aren't just the preserve of Christians, secular clubs and institutions being able to offer us kindness, loyalty helpfulness, purpose and inclusion. As Church, we need to create a different framework, one where we look to God, look out for each other, and consider each other. It's the "more excellent way" required of us, the way of love. Please don't think that I have underestimated the demands made upon us to move in this direction. It looks good on paper, sounds motivating in stirring messages, but the practise of submission to others means having to work hard at it every day!

Our friend was right in upsetting the apple cart (or should that be conker cart?), all those years ago. He opened the way for us to learn about discernment and how not to be afraid to use it. Instead of sitting back and putting teaching on pedestals, because our leader said it, (it must be right!), we need to trust ourselves in discerning Truth, as seen in Jesus. We must guard against organisational pressure, from both local and international sources, arriving in the form of spiritual movements that demand the allegiance we should give to God. We're not infallible, and can either knowingly, or unwittingly, feed gullible people with unwise, and sometimes untruthful ideas or ways in our beliefs and worship practises. We can also ignore suggestions from others because it doesn't "fit in" with whatever plates are being spun at the time. I suppose it amounts to all things being permissible but not all being beneficial, and not imposing our own desires and preferences on each other in God's name. Let's try to ensure that we, as Church, have listening ears and a soft heart, and not just a soft head! Let's also aim to be those people whose words definitely aren't "a load of old conkers", but are words of those who are "more than Conquerors", pointing to the Rowland's Huts of both earth and Heaven!

End of rant. Amen!

Chapter 10: Tying Up The Loose Ends

"These little troubles are getting us ready for an eternal glory that will make all our troubles seem like nothing."
- St. Paul

As a Brownie, I had to get close up and personal with knots. I seemed to be forever wrestling with a sheep shank or a round turn and two half hitches. In trying to crack the conundrum of the reef knot, the compulsion to achieve it had such power as to cause a thousand brownies to wake up out of their sleep, simultaneously sit up in bed and chant, "right over left and left over right. Or is right over left, left over left, right over my shoulder......?" The bits of rope necessary with which to solve those mysteries required the skills of a contortionist. The strands wouldn't stay still and the ends became grubby and frayed with handling. It's much the same with life, our best efforts at keeping things neatly tied up and contained sometimes not being enough. The strands can start to unravel in front of our - and worst of all, other people's eyes, the unravelling often providing the impetus for change and growth. It's only when we lose control that we have to look outside ourselves, hang on tightly, weather the ride, flap our wings - or ride on God's. When it's all too much, we can cry out, asking Him to make us safe, in the Rowland's Hut of His provision, hiding under His wings until we feel strong enough to come out. When we do, we emerge from the shadows to find a new God-shaped space. Experiencing such a time gives us the opportunity to retrace our early steps and influences. It may also enable us to become reconciled with the person we were before life "nobbled" us, when other people's expectations clouded our ability to be who we were created to be.

Canon J. John recently quipped that his mother had been a travel agent for guilt trips! I can totally identify with that sentiment, my own early life having been governed by invisible but effectively controlling strings! The framework of my growing up included the expectation to be self reliant, responsible, a "big girl". In addition, my mother always seemed to feel it necessary to quote the Ten Commandments at me, the effect going deep into my tender soul. It left me with the feeling that I was always responsible - or worse still, guilty, for something I'd done or not done or for someone I'd let down. Any break in proceedings or breathing space for my conscience was all too quickly filled. Those Anglican "sins of commission and omission" had made a well and truly spectacular acquaintance! I now know that the classic cases of false conscience and free floating anxiety had well and truly taken up residence, their effects being far reaching. Like a garden, it's an area I still have to keep tending, spot checking for the weeds that threaten to choke the blossoming flowers of my soul. I so often forget to ask for God's Spirit to alert me to the impending dangers of my faulty thinking. Consequently, I find myself going through the same old motions of wrong perceptions and implications. That pop-up judge, complete with wig and pointy finger, pronounces his verdict before the case has even been brought! However, I don't have to fall for it, as long as I remember to run into that Hut of God's protection. In any case, the battle is only for a short time, Eternally speaking!

The symbolism embodying the re-building of Coventry Cathedral, that of the Phoenix rising out of the ashes, is applicable in the remaking that God wants for us. The charred cross that survived the World War Two bombing of the cathedral was the inspiration for its enduring theme of Reconciliation. Through the channel of its spiritual "heart", the city was encouraged to reach out to the nation whose actions had damaged Coventry's very fabric but not its spirit. This radiated out to all nations and people with its message of renewal, restoration, of making peace with others and ourselves. Forgiveness, as commanded by Jesus, was the active means by which a healing process could take place in the city and its people. It opened the way for new hope, its citizens being able to re establish their lives in peaceful safety. Their newly erected Cathedral, their Rowland's Hut, was the body into which the transplanted "heart" of its City had been placed. Here its worshippers could gather together to feel the collective "heartbeat", to find nourishment and support, and to be sheltered by the God who had never abandoned them in their darkest hours.

There is no greater visual example of the immensity of God in Christ than the tapestry that hangs behind the altar of the Cathedral. Designed and executed by Graham Sutherland measuring seventy five feet by thirty eight feet, It depicts Christ, with the nail marks visible for all to see. It reflects God's glory, the Holy Spirit and The Heavenly Sphere. A human figure, the size of an average man, stands between Christ's feet, the seventy foot difference between Christ and the man acting as a remarkable illustration of His "Overshadowing". It has to be said that the decimation of this city was not exactly on a par with the knotty but smaller problems that we tend to magnify! If the city and its people could pull together to reinstate its proud heritage, then surely we can trust God with our problems. After all, we only have to fix our view on that tapestry!

On a recent trip to Liverpool, my husband and I indulged in a bit of overdue nostalgia. We traced the route that had once been the heartland of Beatle-mania, those city centre streets of "Cavern" fame. Our pop heroes, "The Fab Four" had been the back drop to our youth, we of the Baby Boom generation. Their unsurpassed musical genius, together with their life changing social impact, stand proudly in the cabinet of musical and sociological legend. Our "think of a number, double it, triple it then forget it" stage of life still does nothing to diminish their brilliant contribution to music. Our pilgrimage trail extended from the "Love Me Do" streets of The Beatles to "The Long And Winding Road" of the Anglican Cathedral, unaware that its newest art installation was going to have a profound personal effect. Once inside, my eyes must have been drawn to look upwards and there it was - a pink splash, a gash in that august, majestic temple of worship. Placed just above the door of the west porch, and displayed in Tracey Emin's own handwriting, was a twenty foot neon sign. Entitled "For You", it reads "I felt you and I knew you loved me".

A controversial figure in the art world, Tracey has been regarded by some of having been intentionally salacious. In placing it in a public space where people could contemplate their own feelings, she was indicating that it was meant as a message of love, where people could contemplate their own feelings of love. She wanted it to be open to personal interpretation, leaving it up to the individual to decide whether or not to be "touched by something". Tracey's words stopped me in my tracks with this almost shockingly overt admission. It was a declaration of something usually hidden but secretly hoped for; a felt presence, both in that place and in the outside world. I chose to associate it with the transcendent yet enveloping Presence of God, rather than the love of a more generalised and human kind. It helped define the holy space, giving a new impetus to the Cathedral and its purpose. Rowland's Hut had once more formed itself around me - a small, warm, safe haven of security encased in a huge stone edifice that was dedicated to the out-sized expression of the glory of God. Some lines of an old hymn I used to sing as a Girl Crusader, "In the secret of His Presence, how my soul delights to hide" captures perfectly those pivotal moments in the Cathedral. Fast forwarding a few weeks, all the Mums at the church we attend received a gift of a mirror compact as a Mothering Sunday gift. They were engraved with the words "The God who sees me", the Hebrew name being El Roi. To be made aware that I am seen, known and loved by God is both humbling and reassuring. I will never know if Tracey felt she'd met God, but I feel He'd met her. That brave declaration "writ large", also enabled the likes of me to be acutely aware of God in that place. She may have written the words, but my feeling is that they'd come from the heart of God.

Within the narrative of the Transfiguration of Jesus, there's a little allusion to my now familiar theme. It's to do with Peter - and isn't it always? In his usual "fools rush in where angels fear to tread" manner, he suggested the putting up of three shelters (for those read Rowland-style Huts!) in which to house Jesus, who had been present with them, together with Moses and Elijah, who hadn't, but had put in a sudden guest appearance! I can understand Peter's need to freeze frame the moment. He and his companions were caught up in what the Celtic Christians call a "Thin Place" where Heaven touches Earth. When God spoke, His message was unequivocal. It was a rebuke, a calling back to time and place. No wonder they all fell face down in terror! After all, they'd heard the voice of God! Jesus recognised the shock this caused and started to heal them by exposing and allaying their fear through the gift of His physical touch. You can hardly blame Peter for wanting to stay with his Hero, and wanting to be a faithful friend. One day, he would be with Him - forever! As we cope with our lives on Earth, there are times when we are desperate for the kind of help and rescue that can only come from God. When we feel vulnerable, fragile, fractured or even hopeless, we need Outside help. When it seems too hard to put one foot in front of the other, can't find a way forward or can't climb up from the pit, God has already heard our cry. He's launched the lifeboat and has thrown a rope into the choppy sea or down into that pit. Unlike the rope of my knot tying days, this one won't unravel or fray!

The moment of our human birth propelled us into a strange world. It required us to be separated from the person who had been the source of our previous security and having to learn a whole new set of rules by which to live. Maybe we never totally recover from this somewhat brutal and traumatic beginning. In view of this, it's not surprising that we become distressed by aspects of our human condition, particularly when we're placed in certain situations. We have a mechanism within us known as "fight or flight" and when we're in danger, either real or perceived, it goes into action on our behalf. The trouble is, we can allow it to become over activated so that we can't trust anyone or anything, affecting our relationships, not least with God. When we're in need, He's sometimes the last Person we turn to, instead of the first. It's the hardest thing to try and walk through life on our own, but that wasn't our original design feature. We're meant to be like interlocking jigsaw pieces, joined to other people and covered by the "holy overshadowing". The discovery of a song called "Holy Shadowing" was one of those timely, "meant to be" moments. My husband had tuned into a new Christian television channel and was wading through the mixed bag on offer. All of a sudden, there was this most beautiful song, an affirmation of trust in the refuge that I've been trying to express. The song speaks of mercy, refuge, a hiding place and our shield and glory. In Hebrew, the word to overshadow is Sakak, a word that also means to cover, to huddle together, to be woven and knitted together. I hope you will discover the song, and its significance, for yourself.

God hears all the cries of our hearts. He sees that inner space where we do battle with the pain that besets us. My all time favourite singer-songwriter and word-smith, Paul Simon (okay, one of them!) penned "Homeward Bound". They're the words of a homesick young man, looking out through the window of his soul and craving the familiarity and security that lies on the other side of the water, a place where his thoughts are continually escaping. The person is looking across the sea of his separation, to all that means "home". As we cry to God, our souls are asking for more than the solving of our immediate needs. I believe we're searching for our Heavenly Father's Hut - where we can hide under His Wings.

If I were heading a new chapter, its title would be "To All In-Tents And Purposes"! Although not a chapter, I am leaving the title as a homage to The Keswick Convention, held in, well, Keswick in the English Lake District, and conducted mainly in, well, tents! It's a tribute to the longevity of lifting up God the Father, Son and Spirit through worship, teaching and the fellowship of God's people over the last 140 years. My overview of the Convention leaves me with the conviction that its value lies in the sum being greater than the parts. It provides me with a varied diet of personalities and approaches, enabling me to both enthuse and be enthused, to be inspired, challenged, irritated and perhaps changed by the mix of minds and methods of communication. For me, the greatest gifts are the people I meet and relationships that are initiated, reminding me of those "Hello Man" days as a little girl at my garden gate. It leaves me feeling alive, blessed and fulfilling my true desire. For me, it seems to confirm a purpose for being there, not always found in my everyday existence and certainly not in such concentration. For me, the main tent, with some three thousand worshipping people, is a glimpse of Heaven, again being what the Celtic tradition describes as "The Thin Place" - where Heaven seems to come to the closest point on Earth. For me, it's a chance to let the usual and often paranoid mechanisms of comparing and contrasting my place in society to fall away, if only for a few essential hours, allowing me to align myself with God's Children as I let my accusing inner self have a rest!

Out of this Convention has emerged a fairly recently established arm of expression of the Faith, known by the cleverly inspirational name "Keswick Unconventional", providing a parallel and complementary situation for the expressive arts. It draws upon those musicians, poets, presenters, playwrights and word-smiths whose day jobs are primarily in the world outside the Christian Faith. They collaborate their amazing skills and disciplines to bring life, colour and artistic shape to the spiritual life of the Convention, expanding mind, spirit, emotion and humour, enriching and explaining that which is within us that needs a language and a release, even though the direct words of the Gospel Script may not be articulated but communicated through the spirit of that being expressed. Not all the events are held in tents, the Unconventional being one of them. It takes place on the site of the very first Convention, where a gathering of Christians met on the lawn of the vicarage in 1875. The current vicar is most generous in turning his church building over to the Convention for the best part of a week. It has a welcoming atmosphere, enhanced by the use of fairy lights, a platform with sofas for the presenters and artists and a cafe bar known as MTV, short for the ingeniously named "More Tea Vicar"! It is warm, welcoming and accepting, a refuge, a sanctuary, a true Rowland's Hut of the present moment in my life.

The act of going to the Convention reminds of the Jewish annual pilgrimage to the Temple in Jerusalem. We all must experience the same human situations that they did - the ups and downs, the highs and lows, the ins and outs of living corporately for a length of time with huge swathes of people. Being there does not inoculate us from all the usual major and minor disasters of living. A lovely lady who is a regular attender, is somewhat accident prone. One year she lost her only credit card, whilst another year, it was her car keys. She spent time searching diligently, retracing her steps and pounding the pavements. In losing a contact lens, I had even less chance of retrieval, as three thousand pairs of feet grinding it to dust does not augur well! I am reminded of Mary and Joseph's panic in the loss of their son, Jesus, amongst the crowds of their particular convention - that awful gut wrenching realisation that caused them, like us, to retrace their steps. In finding him, it came as a shock to discover their son's sense of composure and mission. Like us, they were on emotional full alert in their anxiety but unlike us, the outcome acted as a rebuke to their distress. Maybe there's a lesson to be learnt from this! The Convention offers opportunity for both feast and famine in terms of relationship, some wanting more and others needing less. The common bond however, is in the desire to find God at some deeper and more incisive level, the occasion punctuating the year and acting as a crossroads or watershed moment, allowing new decisions to be made in re-orienting our sense of self, our journey and our aims in our attempts to serve God.

The turning of my "memory pages" has made me realise that reviewing and recalling the past has been akin to an archaeological dig, with its "exposure, processing and recording of archaeological remains". It's been an amazing, revealing, and cathartic journey. What was totally unexpected was that once the process had been initiated, the "pages" seemed to turn themselves. It was like wearing a miner's lamp whilst walking through a dark cave, and seeing everything that had been hidden, flooded in light. With a new-found clarity, I began to see that for most of my life, I had allowed a process of shame or failure to shroud my inner self, much like the covering up of furniture and the drawing of curtains in the unused rooms of a stately home. I had unknowingly allowed myself to become a mix of "the Valley of Dry Bones" and a closed suitcase full of unwashed clothes! I needed new life breathing into the bones, and all the contents of the suitcase thrown into a washing machine, before being hung out to be blown in the fresh air. I saw that along the way, I had allowed God to put only patches on my leaking emotions, much like the mending of a puncture, when what was really needed was a completely new "inner-tube". In providing a route I felt able to travel along to the "excavation site". He'd gone before me with a clever plan, as He always does. The path He'd chosen happened to be writing, and through it, He let me dwell in His Heavenly

Rowland's Hut, until I felt safe enough to take a closer look at the things that had been causing a constant "rumbling" in the core of my being.

A description of Christians is that they are Easter people living in a Friday world. So, what are we called to do? We can follow in Rowland's footsteps, seeking to help others move from Friday to Sunday, looking out for the gaps that God may want to fill. Like the political slogan says, We're better together!" God has given us the key to the door of "a Hut with a heart", it's up to us to put the key in the lock and open the door for others to go in, with all their fears and disappointments. Once inside, the hope is that they can start to experience Shalom, God's deep peace, completeness and wholeness. I have been recently made more aware of the movement known as the New Monasticism. A conversation with friends revealed that their son had been greatly helped to find restoration of a life in crisis by such a community, living and working in an environment that promotes the sharing of a common life of prayer, hospitality and work. Friendship and acceptance helps lives to be rebuilt from all forms of brokenness. This, and other such communities, are described as intentional in their rhythm and rule of life, having a concern for, social justice, creation, and creativity, and stressing hospitality and the renouncing of personal wealth. What an example of my Rowland's Hut aspirations!

Biblically, our desire is to be a doorkeeper of His House in Heaven - to rely upon God rather than ourselves. Our job on Earth is to be a welcomer at the door of our own Huts! We can be both a Hut seeker and a Hut provider. My husband and I are grateful for the impact of Rowland's generosity, for literally and metaphorically flinging wide the door of his Hut and for welcoming us all in. As we've journeyed, there have been more Hut moments, time spent with friends and family, a special pastor with respect and generosity of spirit, small groups, worship time at a convention with thousands of people in a tent, and seeing, for just a few moments, a snapshot of Heaven! We're meant for love, to give love and to receive love. Most of all, we are created to love The God who loves us without reserve, and the Son who came to lead us Home. His instruction manual informs us that our rooms are ready and waiting, so I encourage you all to hang on to that promise.

As well as tying up the loose ends, there are the wrongs that need righting, those afflictions of our inner souls and spirits that need to go. A well loved theologian expressed the view that exhaustion of the soul, and its regrets, lead to destruction We all need a route we can take, and a process by which we can evaluate ourselves, and offload those internal slag heaps that build up, causing us pain and weighing us down. Our best route is that road to God, where we can meet Him in the Divine Exchange, that place where, with great relief, we can wait on Him, confessing those things that have brought us to a grinding halt and that have made us feel unworthy of Him and others. Psalm Thirty Four tells us that His ears and eyes are alert to the cries of the righteous, and He delivers them from their troubles. When our inner "magnetic needle" seems to be spinning round without direction, He re-orientates us, readjusting and re calibrating our focus and our hearts, giving us peace and new purposes. We wonder how God can see any significance in the ordinariness of who we are, but like the knots of my Brownie days, God wants to come "up close and personal". It's like logging on to Google Earth on our computers, where the "world" spins and starts to come closer, and as it does so, the flattened shapes take on contour until the chosen destination is revealed in its entirety. That's exactly what God does with us, whether we perceive it or not. He comes that close!

Sometimes God gives us something which is ultimately going to be for our good, but which initially seems totally alien. It's like Abraham being told that he was being given Canaan as a sign of God's covenant, where he would live as an alien, in an alien land. Our whole landscape can feel wrong, but God can make it right for our, and His higher purposes, despite it feeling the exact opposite, and appearing like a photo negative, everything seeming reversed - white and black, black and white, right and left, left and right. We're told in Jeremiah that "Cursed is the one who trusts in man....whose heart turns from the Lord....He will dwell in the parched lands of the desert, in a salt land where no-one lives. But blessed is the man who trusts in the Lord....He will be like a tree planted by the water that sends out its roots by the stream....its leaves are always green....it never fails to bear fruit". The phrase "in a salt land" resonates in my soul, and is on a par with the desert imagery, illustrating how it feels when we're out of joint with God, and ourselves. You can feel the impact of a place where a high degree of piled up salt renders the area inhospitable and uninhabitable, stunting and stopping growth of any type. We can choose not to stay in this place by allowing God to perform a spiritual clear out, painful and unnerving though this might be. Preferring to keep what's familiar, we can enter into a kind of tug of war with ourselves, but there needs to be a winner, and God wants it to be us. We need to let Him do the necessary work, so that in His wisdom, He'll find a way that is unique to each of us, in order to help us.

In starting the process of righting the wrongs of my own life, the route has been through the act of writing, a literal case of "writing the wrongs", giving me the opportunity to look backwards, and gain a new perspective. I hope that you will have the courage to exchange the wisdom we think we have, for the wisdom God certainly has. Why? It's because He loves us, and wants the best for us. Once we stop thinking we know best, who wouldn't? Why wouldn't we? Please try it, and discover your brand new place in His Perfect Rowland's Hut!